San Francisco

THEN AND NOW

San Francisco

THEN AND NOW

Dennis Evanosky
and Eric J. Kos

THUNDER BAY
P · R · E · S · S

San Diego, California

Thunder Bay Press
An imprint of the Baker & Taylor Publishing Group
THUNDER BAY 10350 Barnes Canyon Road, San Diego, CA 92121
P · R · E · S · S www.thunderbaybooks.com

Produced by Salamander Books,
an imprint of Anova Books Ltd.
10 Southcombe Street, London W14 0RA, UK

"Then and Now" is a registered trademark of Anova Books Ltd.

© 2010 Salamander Books

ISBN-13: 978-1-60710-195-6
ISBN-10: 1-60710-195-5

The Library of Congress has catalogued the original Thunder Bay edition as follows:

Evanosky, Dennis.
  San Francisco then & now / Dennis Evanosky and Eric J. Kos.
    p. cm.
  ISBN-13: 978-1-60710-003-4
  ISBN-10: 1-60710-003-7
  1. San Francisco (Calif.)--Pictorial works. 2. San Francisco (Calif.)--History--
Pictorial works. 3. Historic buildings--California--San Francisco--Pictorial works.
4. Architecture--California--San Francisco--Pictorial works. 5. San Francisco (Calif.)--
Buildings, structures, etc.--Pictorial works. 6. Repeat photography--California--San
Francisco. I. Kos, Eric J. II. Title. III. Title: San Francisco then and now.
  F869.S343E93 2009
  979.4'6104--dc22
                        2009016769

1 2 3 4 5 14 13 12 11 10

Printed in China

Dennis and Eric dedicate this book to Karl Mondon, our friend and
photographer extraordinaire.

ACKNOWLEDGMENTS
The authors would like to thank Library Director Patricia Keats at the
Society of California Pioneers and the staff of the Daniel E. Koshland
San Francisco History Center at the San Francisco Public Library for
their assistance in obtaining the historical photographs for this book.

PICTURE CREDITS
The publisher wishes to thank the following for kindly supplying the
photographs that appear in this book:

"Then" photographs:
All "Then" images in the book were supplied courtesy of San Francisco
History Center, San Francisco Public Library, except for the following:
Society of California Pioneers: pages 12 main, 22, 26, 36, 40, 42, 62, 64,
66, 68, 76 inset, 78 main, 88, 102, 104, 108, 116, 124, 126.
Library of Congress: pages 12 inset (HABS CAL,38-SANFRA,9-3), 52 (cph
3c15228), 54–55 top (6a02003u), 56 main (HABS CAL,38-SANFRA,58-2),
94–95 top (LC-DIG-ppmsca-07588), 130 (LC-USZ62-70342).
Ted Streshinsky/Corbis: page 134.

"Now" photographs:
All "Now" images were taken by Karl Mondon.

Introduction

The year 1776 represents an auspicious time in American history. An often overlooked event that occurred on the West Coast that year was the first European settlement at the future site of the city of San Francisco. In the name of the Spanish crown, Mission San Francisco de Asís and the Presidio (Spanish for "fort") were established there. The Spanish chose to consecrate the mission near an already popular spot.

The Yelamu tribe, one of fifty independent Ohlone tribes, had settled nearby thousands of years earlier. Small groups settled at the water's edge all along the bay, where Crissy Field, the Sutro Baths, and Fort Mason would one day reside. Shallow Mission Bay, the nearest encroachment of the bay waters to the eventual site of the mission, teemed with edible fish and birds. A nearby stream provided fresh water for a thriving settlement of these Native Americans.

A world apart from these people practicing their peaceful existence in an isolated location, Europeans slowly encroached on them. Spanish explorers and plenty of other sailors had gone right past the foggy hills and missed the 4,200-foot gap of the Golden Gate for more than a century. In the end, a land expedition discovered San Francisco Bay.

The expedition of Don Gaspar de Portola saw the waters first in 1769. To combat any other imperial designs, in 1775 the Spanish empire aimed to colonize the Bay Area. They sent a company under the command of Captain Juan Bautista de Anza from Sonora, Mexico, with 240 settlers and soldiers. Once they reached the headlands of the Presidio the following year, not only did the expedition survive, it had grown by three members. In September they dedicated the Presidio, and a month later, Mission San Francisco was born.

Until 1849, the city remained an isolated outpost—a quiet anchorage with little supply and few exports. A visit from the British flagship *Discovery* in 1792 brought Sir George Vancouver to town. He set up a base for pioneers, traders, and explorers. Thirty years later, merchant William Richardson drew a map to a cove near the village, a safer haven than anchoring in the surf off the Presidio. On his map he called the community Yerba Buena, after a plentiful native mint.

By 1846 the town had grown to fifty buildings and became a target for American forces fighting in the Mexican War. Commodore J. B. Montgomery and the sailors aboard the USS *Portsmouth* claimed the city for the United States. The following year, the town's *alcalde*, or mayor, Washington Bartlett, rechristened his city San Francisco.

An event in 1848 turned San Francisco upside down. In January, James Marshall discovered a shiny yellow metal in the creek of a sawmill he was building. He didn't think much of it at first. But word slowly spread, and by December, President James K. Polk announced the discovery of gold in California. The rush was on. Some 80,000 new residents arrived within a year, from nearly every country in the world.

The city first expanded into Noe Valley, along the eastern coast and up the side of Telegraph Hill. By 1855 the city burst its seams again and alderman and milkman Charles H. Gough was given the task of laying out the new Western Addition neighborhood that had grown west of Larkin Street. Three years later, officials extended the city again, naming the new main street after a former San Francisco mayor, James Van Ness.

In 1860 the city saw its first horse-drawn rail line set up by the Market Street Railroad Company. Andrew Hallidie introduced the famous cable car in 1873, making steep hills like Nob and Russian available for settlement. The 1870 census reported the city's population at 150,000, with new forms of transportation spurring growth. After two decades, the population doubled.

The city continued to add new neighborhoods, and by the turn of the century, it reached Divisidero Street in the west and Thirtieth Street in the south. Just then, one of the most significant events in the city's history changed the lives of hundreds of thousands of San Franciscans: the Great Earthquake and Fire of 1906. It was not so much the quake but the fire that destroyed homes and businesses and claimed about 3,000 lives. Intrepid San Franciscans rebuilt the city with vigor, setting off a building boom. By the time the Panama-Pacific Exposition brought 8.5 million international visitors in 1915, San Francisco was vibrant, bustling, and wealthy again.

In 1918 the Twin Peaks Tunnel opened, allowing the creation of western neighborhoods like the Sunset District, Forest Hill, and Balboa Terrace. These helped double the city's population again to its current level of just over 800,000.

The city contributed its part to the World Wars, serving as a shipping point for the Pacific theater, but during those times, expansion of the city stalled.

Boom times in the 1950s brought expansion upward again. The first skyscrapers arrived on San Francisco's skyline, to the point that in the late 1960s residents began to complain of the "Manhattanization" of San Francisco. A new generation had risen, and the hippies gathering in numbers near the intersection of Haight and Ashbury called for a more natural existence.

Another temblor shook the city in October 1989, interrupting the third game of the World Series between the San Francisco Giants and the Oakland Athletics at Candlestick Park. The magnitude-6.9 Loma Prieta earthquake caused widespread damage in the area and resulted in the enactment of further safety measures for buildings.

Digital prosperity brought revitalization to the South of Market neighborhood, previously an industrial area. The Yerba Buena Gardens complex, Museum of Modern Art, and AT&T Park serve as reminders of this rebirth. City hall reopened in 1999 after an earthquake retrofit, putting a cap on the city's new gilded age.

The city enriched its cultural tradition with the reopening of the De Young Museum in 2005 and the California Academy of Sciences in 2008, both in Golden Gate Park. Today, the city continues its long history of entrepreneurship and free-spirited thinking. San Francisco, then as now, remains a captivating place that calls to everyone in the world for a fortune, or just a visit.

FORT POINT

An organized swim across
the Golden Gate in 1911

The U.S. Army built Fort Point between 1853 and 1861 in the Third System style of military architecture. The army designed the fort to accommodate 126 cannons. Company I of the Third U.S. Artillery Regiment garrisoned the fort in February 1861. Union forces occupied the fort throughout the Civil War, but the advent of faster, more powerful rifled cannons made brick forts such as Fort Point obsolete. In 1886 the army withdrew its troops; fourteen years later it removed the last cannon. This photo shows an organized swim across the Golden Gate on August 20, 1911. Four women and several men attempted the swim. A crowd of 5,000 watched Nita Sheffield and her sister Lyba, Nellie Schmidt, and Terie Desch. Nellie finished in forty-two minutes; Lyba was just one minute behind her. Nita reached the Marin shore in forty-six minutes; Terie gave up a hundred yards from her goal. None of the men finished the race.

Original plans for the construction of the Golden Gate Bridge called for Fort Point's demolition. However, bridge builder Joseph Strauss considered Fort Point such an important thread in San Francisco's fabric that he designed a special arch over the fort. This allowed him to build the bridge without destroying the fort. While the fort buildings are obscured here, they can be seen clearly from alternative viewing points (see page 9). Strauss used Fort Point as a base of operations for the construction of the bridge, which was completed in May 1937. During World War II, about 100 soldiers occupied Fort Point. They manned searchlights and rapid-fire cannons, an integral part of a submarine net strung across the entrance to the bay. Civil War reenactors frequently bring the fort to life, evoking the memory of the bastion's nineteenth-century importance. Fort Point became a National Historic Site on October 16, 1970.

GOLDEN GATE BRIDGE

The longest-spanning suspension bridge in the world at the time of its opening in 1937

Left: The first proposal to build a bridge spanning the Golden Gate came from the self-proclaimed "Emperor of the United States," Norton I, a bankrupt gold miner who lost his mind and began passing edicts backed with little authority during the 1860s. Railroad baron Charles Crocker may have liked the crazy idea, and in the 1870s he drew up plans for a bridge that were never used. Automobiles and the modern age brought the issue to the fore when North Bay commuters lost patience with the long ferry ride to the city. Adding momentum perhaps was Chicago engineer Joseph B. Strauss, in town for the Panama-Pacific Exposition of 1915. Strauss's Aeroscope, a 700-ton engineering masterpiece, took 118 fairgoers at a time to 330 feet, the ideal height from which to view the bridgeless Golden Gate. In 1917 San Francisco engaged the accomplished engineer to span the gate. In all, Strauss completed more than 400 bridges in various parts of the world during his lifetime.

Above: The Golden Gate Bridge must withstand 100-mph winds that can cause the middle of the span to sway up to twenty-one feet. One of the towers, as tall as a sixty-five-story building, is anchored 1,215 feet from the shore, where it suffers the pressure of a 7.5-knot tidal outrush during ebb tide, backed by the swift running waters of the Sacramento and San Joaquin rivers. During flood tide, the tower subsists under the full weight of the Pacific Ocean. Temperature variations cause the steel structure to grow ten feet taller when warmed in the sun. Strauss carefully incorporated all of these considerations into the engineering of the structure. Built between 1933 and 1937, its 4,200-foot span made it the longest suspension bridge in the world at that time. The last voter-approved bond financing the bridge's construction was paid off in 1971; since then, tolls collected cover maintenance, including a never-ending paint job in international orange. Today more than 100,000 cars cross the bridge daily.

PRESIDIO AVENUE GATES

The Spanish chose this spot to protect their interests in Alta California

Left: In this 1898 photograph, soldiers wait at the gates of the Presidio above San Francisco Bay. The Spanish chose this strategic spot to build a fort to protect their interests in the far northern reaches of Alta California. The Spanish usually built a presidio, or garrison, to house their soldiers; a mission to house priests whose "mission" it was to convert the native peoples; and a pueblo, or village, to house their citizens. They chose not to build a pueblo at this outpost; there was one in San Jose. The Spanish lost their North American power base in 1821 when they were ousted from Mexico. The Mexican government abandoned the presidio in 1833, leaving for their outpost in Sonoma. Finally, the government decided to found a pueblo here. In 1834 they elected Don Francisco de Haro as its first alcalde, a post similar to mayor. A year later, Richard Henry Dana showed up aboard the *Pilgrim*. Dana's book *Two Years Before the Mast* enticed many Yankees to visit San Francisco.

Above: Today's Presidio presents a different picture than the military post of the past. Its 1,491 acres include a shoreline with coastal bluffs, hilltops and gardens, Mountain Lake, and Baker Beach with its breathtaking view of the Golden Gate. The Presidio's key points of interest include the Main Post, the historic heart of the place, where the Spanish set down roots in 1776. The Letterman District, where Letterman Hospital once stood, is home to the twenty-three-acre Letterman Digital Arts Center. A fountain dedicated to the beloved Jedi master Yoda presides over the home of Lucasfilm, the company that introduced the world to heroes like Indiana Jones and Luke Skywalker and villains like Jabba the Hutt and Darth Vader. The center houses Lucasfilm Ltd., Industrial Light and Magic, and LucasArts under one roof.

BLACK POINT

Site of the city's first jail, the brig *Euphemia*

Left: Black Point drew its name from the laurel trees, which, in contrast to the golden grassland, must have appeared black to passing ships. The land formed a harbor, which served as an anchorage for the city's first jail, the brig *Euphemia*, seen in the center of this photo. Abandoned ships were quickly put to new uses in the 1850s. Later, John Frémont, one of California's first senators, lived at the very tip of Black Point. Another senator, David Broderick, died in a home here in 1859 after suffering a wound in a duel. Once Frémont went to fight in the Civil War, the tip of the point became a battery designed to protect against Confederate raids on shipping. After the earthquake of 1906, Black Point became a temporary home to many displaced San Franciscans. By then, the battery grew into Fort Mason, headquarters of the western armies. By the 1920s, industrial and military uses had encroached on the shoreline (see inset). Lower Fort Mason became a base for embarkation during both World Wars.

Above: This is the site of today's Aquatic Park with its Streamline Moderne Maritime Museum. Aquatic Pier stretches out into the bay—a place for recreation, fishing, and incredible views. Fort Mason only echoes of men leaving for war; today, the army rents much of it out after almost of century of active use. Only some of the former officer housing remains in use by the army, with the remainder serving as private homes. A mix of parks, gardens, and trails grace the highlands of Black Point today, offering sweeping views north to Alcatraz and west to the Golden Gate Bridge. Fort Mason Center has been converted to provide space for nonprofit and cultural activities. The former military installation now hosts three dozen nonprofit organizations, including three museums, six theaters, and the City College of San Francisco's Art Campus. In recent years, more than 15 million people have attended more than 15,000 events at Fort Mason, including the 2008 YouTube Live event.

CRISSY FIELD

This former airfield was closed prior to the construction of the Golden Gate Bridge

This 1938 photograph shows soldiers camping on Crissy Field when it was part of the Presidio. Native Americans once gathered at this spot, which later became a post for Russian, English, and American traders. Part of the Panama-Pacific International Exposition was held here in 1915. When it ended, the U.S. Army converted the place into an airfield, the Flying Field at the Presidio. Major Henry "Hap" Arnold—the only officer to ever hold the grade of five-star general in both the U.S. Army and Air Force— was not happy with the name. He successfully lobbied to change the name to Crissy Field in honor of Major Dana H. Crissy, who crashed and died on October 8, 1919, while attempting to land in Salt Lake City. San Francisco Bay's fog often meant poor flying conditions. In 1936 Hamilton Field opened in Marin County. The handwriting was on the wall; pilots knew that flying would become more difficult when the Golden Gate Bridge was built nearby. Crissy Field closed as an air base before the bridge opened.

Today's Crissy Field boasts the Golden Gate Promenade, which provides access to a restored tidal marsh and beach. Runners, cyclists, and folks just out for a stroll can enjoy some of the world's most famous views, including the Golden Gate Bridge, Alcatraz and Angel islands, and the Marin County shore. Nearby Crissy Field Center's facilities include a media lab, resource library, arts workshop, science lab, gathering room, and teaching kitchen in addition to a café and bookstore. The center is housed in the Presidio's 1939 commissary—a food store for military personnel and their families. The building was left vacant in the 1970s when the military downsized its operations on the Presidio. In 2000 it saw new life as the Crissy Field Center.

MARINA DISTRICT

This area of the city bore the brunt of the 1989 Loma Prieta earthquake

Above: The Palace of Fine Arts stands out in the background of this photograph showing firefighters in the Marina District coping with the aftermath of the Loma Prieta earthquake. It was just after 5:00 p.m. on October 17, 1989, and the third game of the World Series was about to get underway at San Francisco's Candlestick Park— a dream series that pitted the Oakland Athletics against the San Francisco Giants, billed as "the Battle of the Bay." At 5:04 the earth shook for an interminable fifteen seconds. Frightened fans and players quickly left the ballpark. Some went home to San Francisco's Marina District to learn that their neighborhood had suffered the brunt of the temblor, whose epicenter was seventy miles to the south, near Loma Prieta Peak. Liquefaction of the underlying landfill caused homes—many built with "soft stories," ground-level stories with little support—to collapse. Pipes carrying natural gas ruptured and fires broke out.

Right: Twenty years have passed and the Marina District has returned to normal. Many of the homes still rest on soft stories as city leaders struggle with ways to shore up any future damage. Most of the homes in the district date back to the 1920s, a heady time after the 1915 closing of the Panama-Pacific International Exposition left plenty of real estate in the district to blanket with homes. The Marina Development Corporation stepped into an area some called Harbor View; others dubbed it the North End. They created 634 residential lots and the Marina Green, a favorite spot for flying kites and windsurfing because gusts of wind here often blow in at fifty miles an hour. The district also boasts another popular destination: the Exploratorium—the ideal place to literally get your hand onto science—located inside the Palace of Fine Arts.

PALACE OF FINE ARTS

Originally constructed for the Panama-Pacific International Exposition of 1915

Left: The Panama-Pacific International Exposition of 1915 was a tremendous success. Money poured into the local economy along with tourists from the world over, helping San Francisco bounce back from the damage caused by the earthquake and fire of 1906. General Electric did all the lighting for the event, which brings Bernard Maybeck's Palace of Fine Arts to life in this photograph taken just after its completion. The fairgrounds encompassed seventy-six city blocks and earned the moniker "Dome City" due to its many original domed buildings, including the Palace of Fine Arts, the Palace of Varied Industries, the Manufacturers Palace, the Liberal Arts Palace, and the Palace of Horticulture. Many of these were constructed with a plasterlike material designed to last just for the duration of the fair. When the Palace of Fine Arts in all its beauty wasn't torn down, some wondered how long it would remain standing. Parts of the building collapsed and workers completely rebuilt the structure in the 1960s.

Above: Immediately following the exposition, the Palace of Fine Arts became a rotating exhibit hall. During World War II, every public building became fair game, and the army commandeered the palace for the storage of jeeps and tanks. Maybeck intended for the reflecting lagoon to not only reflect the beauty of the palace but also to provide an ample distance from which to view the impressive building. Many have viewed the Palace of Fine Arts from even farther away once it graced the Hollywood screen. Director Alfred Hitchcock used the Bay Area as a shooting ocation for several films, and the Palace of Fine Arts appears in his classic film *Vertigo*. It also appeared in The Rock during the 1990s. In recent years, the Exploratorium has continued to maintain the palace and hold concerts, special exhibits, movies, art programs, and educational events there while welcoming about half a million visitors annually.

SAN FRANCISCO BAY

Skyscrapers have replaced the masts on the city's skyline

Left: This picture of San Francisco Bay dates to 1850, when San Francisco was scarcely the world-class city we know today. A contemporary described it as "the cluster of houses between Telegraph Hill and El Rincon." According to this writer, "The Presidio was reduced to two dilapidated adobe buildings, in which was quartered a United States military company. The Mission was a resort where it was pleasant to while away a Sunday." The writer could have added something about the lack of men in the city; they were all in the gold fields. Some arrived by ship and everyone aboard, from the cabin boy to the captain, jumped ship for richer diggings than they would ever find in San Francisco. Those "sticks" in the distance are the masts of just some of the ships that these prospectors abandoned on their way to seek their riches. This is the oldest known photograph of San Francisco.

Above: Skyscrapers, which include the 493-foot Hilton San Francisco (left), have replaced the masts on the city's skyline. The city rose from the ashes more than once in the mid-nineteenth century, and it is no accident that the city chose a phoenix as a symbol. The "Christmas Eve Fire" struck in 1849, leaving $1 million in damage in its wake. Three fires wreaked havoc in 1851. The May 4 conflagration started at Portsmouth Square, the city's heart; it spread north toward Broadway and south to Pine Street. Just a month later on June 14, another fire struck. This one spread along the old shoreline west toward Battery Street. Eight days later, a third fire damaged the same area as the May 4 conflagration.

SHAG ROCK

Shipping hazard blown to bits

Left: Shag Rock, named for the shag birds that frequented the rock's pinnacle, was blown up in 1901 to rid sea captains of this impediment to their shipping. The Army Corps of Engineers waged a campaign against such impediments, though at least one early seafaring photographer took an image of Fort Point from Shag Rock; Harding Rock can be seen in the distance. Both of these pinnacles stood out from the water, while others lurked dangerously just below the surface. A photographer, knowing the precise time of the explosion, caught tiny bits of Shag Rock and many gallons of water being blown hundreds of feet into the air. Looking north over the bay, the photographer also caught Alcatraz and Angel Island to the right, which appear to be dwarfed by the column of water. The highest point of Angel Island is Mount Livermore at 781 feet. Well in the distance at left is Marin County's Mount Tamalpais, which rises 2,571 feet.

Above: Rocks lurking just below San Francisco Bay's surface caused many problems for ship captains since the first record of Blossom Rock in 1826. The hazard took its name from the British navy's HMS *Blossom*, which ran afoul of them just southeast of Alcatraz. Northwest of Alcatraz, Shag Rock, Harding Rock, and Arch Rock each needed blasting as well. The rocks were blasted over the years as technology allowed ship hulls to sink deeper into the water. Blossom Rock suffered the first blast of dynamite in 1869. At the beginning of the twentieth century, they were all blasted to a depth of thirty feet below the waterline. In the 1930s, Blossom Rock was taken down to forty feet below the waterline and the others to thirty-five feet below the waterline. More blasting is proposed to lower all the rocks to a depth of forty feet. Today, looking north over San Francisco Bay to Richardson Bay and beyond reveals some of the most valuable property in the nation in the cities of Tiburon, Belvedere, and Sausalito.

ALCATRAZ

Alcatraz was the most expensive prison to operate in the United States

Left: According to the information on the back of the photograph, the guard is standing near the cells where he foiled an escape attempt. Unlike other federal penitentiaries where prisoners were housed two, three, or four to a cell and better-behaved inmates lived in dormitories, Alcatraz inmates were housed one person to a cell. In other penitentiaries in the federal system, inmates spent most of their day outside their cells. At Alcatraz, inmates had to earn their way out of their cells through good behavior. Alcatraz was the most expensive prison to operate in the United States—three times more expensive to operate than any other federal prison. By the 1960s, other, more modern institutions were able to serve the same purpose for less cost. The penitentiary closed on March 21, 1963. Nine years later, Congress created the Golden Gate National Recreation Area, which included Alcatraz. The island opened for public tours in the fall of 1973.

Above: Tourists replace the guard in this photograph taken inside the Alcatraz prison. Visitors from all over the world can step onto Alcatraz and experience each period of the small island's history, including what remains of the Civil War–era fortress. The National Park Service, which maintains "the Rock," has staged Civil War reenactments on Alcatraz. Visitors also learn about the 1969–71 American Indian occupation of the island, and still see the graffiti the Indians left on the penitentiary's walls. Most of all, tourists come to learn about Alcatraz the penitentiary. They listen intently to stories about Al Capone and "the Birdman," Robert Stroud. They ask to see where Machine-Gun Kelly spent his days and quietly follow tour guides around as they speak of day-to-day life on the Rock. Alcatraz has been popular with Hollywood, too: Clint Eastwood starred in two movies featuring Alcatraz, The Enforcer and Escape from Alcatraz; and Sean Connery and Nicolas Cage teamed up in The Rock.

MEIGG'S WHARF / PIER 39

Named for Henry Meiggs, lumberman, promoter, rail baron, and con man

Left: New York lumberman Henry Meiggs sailed to San Francisco in 1849 with a hull packed with fresh-cut Catskill lumber. In a city whose population went from 1,500 to 15,000 seemingly overnight, the lumber sold at twenty times its East Coast value. With the instant fortune, Meiggs built a wharf (shown here in 1865) that jutted 2,000 feet out into the bay—a marvel of engineering at the time—and began speculating on real estate in the area. He attempted to encourage ship captains to dock at his wharf rather than at the old Yerba Buena harbor, which was shallow and unfavorable to shipping. Like so many whose wealth came easy, Meiggs overextended himself rapidly. In the untamed city, rampant corruption delivered a valuable document to Meiggs just when he needed it. The booklet contained blank warrants against the city's Street Fund, which the mayor and controller had foolishly signed in advance. The fund had no money at the time, but many unsuspecting investors weren't aware and bought Meiggs's fraudulent notes anyway.

Above: Meiggs's jig was up when buyers attempted to cash in the warrants, only to find the Street Department had nothing to pay. He skipped town in 1854 and landed in South America with $8,000 in ill-gotten investments. Henry Meiggs, lumberman, promoter, and con man, was about to add another title: railroad baron. He lost the $8,000 on speculation and had to pawn his watch, which financed railroad exploits in Chile and Costa Rica and a career as "Don Enrique," the veritable dictator of Peru. Meiggs amassed a fortune of about $100,000 by completing government projects of his own design. He supposedly paid back all of his San Francisco creditors. While he never returned to California and lost his fortune again, in 1873 he convinced the California State Legislature to pass a bill making it illegal to try him for crimes committed before 1855. In all, Meiggs's only regret was selling his watch. Today, the location of Meiggs's Wharf plays host to Fisherman's Wharf and Piers 39 and 41, which are among the most-visited locations in town.

CABLE CAR ON HYDE STREET

The Hyde Street cable car line dates back to 1890

Left: A cable car descends Hyde Street on the way to its terminal next to the Hyde Street Pier and the ferry to Sausalito. In the background, the aircraft carrier USS Ticonderoga steams home to Alameda, the East Bay's island city. The carrier saw action in World War II, including at Pearl Harbor on December 7, 1941. Alameda Naval Air Station was the *Ticonderoga*'s home port in 1957, about when this photograph was taken. While many other cities across the United States suffered decay and population loss during the suburbanization of the 1950s, San Francisco bucked the trend. Its geography gives the city a dense, compact nature that prevents the Los Angeles–style sprawl that claimed so many other urban centers. San Francisco tore up many streetcar tracks, preferring the more modern subway and bus systems. But the city's close-knit nature, diverse culture, and strong middle class helped maintain a vibrant urban lifestyle that was disappearing from many other great cities in the nation at the time.

Above: The Hyde Street cable car line dates back to 1890, when the California Street Cable Railroad, or "Cal Cable," opened the O'Farrell, Jones, and Hyde lines. Only the Hyde Street line remains in operation today. The concept of progress threatened the cable car several times in San Francisco. In 1947 Mayor Roger Lapham proposed scrapping the city-owned Powell Street line in favor of hill-climbing buses. San Francisco rose up in defiance, and Lapham was soon voted out of office. Despite this early victory, the California Street Cable Railroad went broke in 1951. Desperate negotiations resulted in the city and county taking over the assets of Cal Cable and successfully operating the lines ever since. The Hyde Street line carried passengers from Powell and Market streets to the Hyde Street Pier, effectively connecting some of the city's financial and shopping districts to Sausalito via ferry. Once at the Hyde Street Pier, other ferries could be taken to Vallejo, Tiburon, Alcatraz, or Angel Island at docks nearby.

HYDE STREET PIER

Now home to the Maritime National Historic Park

Above: In this 1938 photograph, cars line up on the Hyde Street Pier, awaiting the ferries to carry them to Sausalito and Berkeley. Before the Bay Bridge opened in 1936 and cars started flowing across the Golden Gate Bridge the following year, the Hyde Street Pier served commuters as the principal automobile ferry terminal connecting Sausalito in Marin County and Berkeley in the East Bay with San Francisco. Golden Gate Ferries, a subsidiary of the Southern Pacific Railroad, operated the ferries from the Hyde Street Pier, which the federal government had designated a part of U.S. Highways 101 and 40. The Hyde Street Pier was built in 1922 and service lasted until 1941.

Right: On April 18, 1961, the State Division of Beaches and Parks and the San Francisco Port Authority signed a lease that would transform the Hyde Street Pier into a replica of an old-time wharf. The San Francisco Maritime Museum Association oversaw the project, which reshaped the old working Hyde Street Pier into a museum. The pier is now home to the Maritime National Historic Park and its historic vessels. Five ships—the 1886 square-rigger *Balclutha*, the 1890 steam ferryboat *Eureka*, the 1891 scow schooner *Alma*, the 1895 schooner *C.A. Thayer*, and the 1915 steam schooner *Wapama*—arrived at the pier in October 1963. (All but the *Wapama* remain at the pier; it is now docked in Richmond, California.) In 1978 the pier joined the National Park Service when it became part of the Golden Gate National Recreational Area. The pier became a separate national park in 1989. Visitors to the Hyde Street Pier can enjoy activities such as children's outings and boatbuilding and woodworking classes.

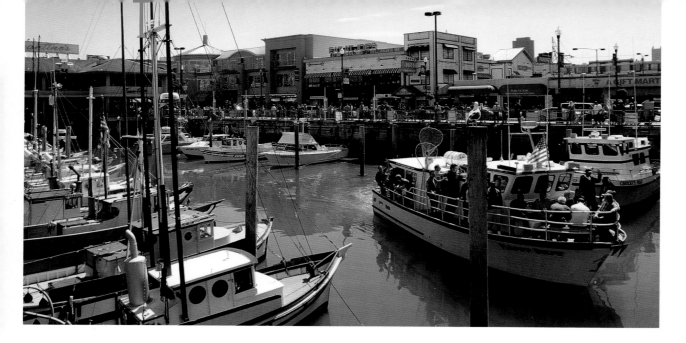

FISHERMAN'S WHARF

Seafaring life continues alongside the tourist trade at today's Fisherman's Wharf

Left: Just as its name implies, Fisherman's Wharf is a working wharf and home to a fleet of fishing vessels. Monterey fishing boats like these have been procuring San Francisco's seafood (including Dungeness crab) since the mid-nineteenth century. Italian gold miners didn't have much luck panning the riverbeds, so they turned to one of their traditional skills, fishing, and settled near Meiggs's Wharf. Later, seafood restaurants with names like Alioto's and Nick's began pulling in gold for the Italians. Another Italian added flavor to the wharf—chocolate. Domingo Ghirardelli came to San Francisco in 1849 seeking gold. He did not have much luck either, so instead opened a store in Stockton, California. There he sold confections and other specialties to miners out of a tent. After raising enough capital, he opened his chocolate factory at the western end of the wharf area in 1852. The Ghirardelli name has become synonymous with chocolate and San Francisco ever since. The company claims it was the first to bring chocolate into common use in the United States.

Above: Fisherman's Wharf's industry has branched out into the tourist trade. While Meiggs's original construction was rebuilt around 1900, the character of seafaring life hasn't changed much. Fishermen continue family traditions aboard their grandfathers' fishing vessels while near the docks fishmongers skillfully crack freshly caught crabs, withdrawing all the meat from their shells in mere seconds. After tourists fill their bellies with seafood at one of thirteen full-service restaurants on Pier 39, they can fill their days with endless attractions. With more than 110 shops, the sea lions that commandeer K Dock, the San Francisco Wax Museum, ferries to Alcatraz and Angel Island, the USS *Pampanito* (a preserved D-day submarine), Ghirardelli Square, and still more attractions, tourists have plenty to choose from at Fisherman's Wharf. Street performances are common in the area: impromptu musical acts, clowns, mimes, caricaturists, and chalk muralists display their talents in hopes of earning some spare change.

LOMBARD STREET

The "crookedest street" in San Francisco

Left: Early property owners realized that they could get more for their money with larger tracts of land to sell if they laid out boundaries in straight lines, no matter the geography. The result: some very steep property boundaries and streets, one of them Lombard Street on Russian Hill. This 1922 photograph shows the transformation of Lombard Street into one of the premier tourist attractions in San Francisco—the "crookedest street." When they created this anomaly, city engineers had no intention of turning this stretch of road into a tourist attraction; they were simply trying to provide a safer way down the extraordinarily steep slope that Lombard Street was forced to traverse on Russian Hill. To achieve this, they crammed eight cobblestone switchbacks into the street's incline between Leavenworth Street at the base and Hyde Street at the top of the slope. The engineers realized that pedestrians are much more agile than automobiles, so they designed stairways without curves on either side of the street.

Above: The speed limit is five miles per hour on this one-way street. It's all downhill and it's all very crooked: Lombard between Leavenworth and Hyde makes every tourist's must-walk-up, must-drive-down list. (One San Franciscan suggests a taxi ride down the hill at night for an experience that the tourist will talk about for a long time.) Another tourist treat involves two of San Francisco's attractions: catch the Hyde Street cable car at Powell and Market streets, get off at Lombard, and walk down to Leavenworth. There's more to Lombard Street than this crookedest stretch. The street begins in the Presidio, traverses Cow Hollow, Russian Hill, Telegraph Hill, and ends at the Embarcadero. For much of that distance, it's not very crooked. And despite all the hoopla, Lombard Street between Hyde and Leavenworth is not really San Francisco's crookedest street. That honor goes to Vermont Street where it runs along McKinley Square in the Potrero District, well off the tourist trade's beaten path.

TELEGRAPH HILL

Home to Coit Tower, built in 1933 as a tribute to San Francisco's firefighters

Left: A telescope sits atop Telegraph Hill, home to Coit Tower today, in this photograph taken during the Civil War. The hill long served as an observation point. In 1846 Captain John Montgomery claimed San Francisco for the United States and called for a defensive structure on the hill. He also had a signaling device constructed there to alert him to vessels entering the Golden Gate. The mechanical device had arms and worked much like semaphore: depending on the arms' position, observers below could discern what type of ship was entering the bay. For years, merchants, financiers, speculators, and others used the signal to meet an expected ship just as it appeared at the dock. Known variously as Loma Alta and Prospect Hill, the site took its current name during the last quarter of the nineteenth century when a telegraph office on the hill took signals from the electric telegraph at Point Lobos and sent information on arriving ships to subscribers in the city below.

Above: Lillie Hitchcock Coit had a colorful life. As a fifteen-year-old in 1858, she contributed her enormous spirit and tiny efforts to putting out fires with the Knickerbocker Engine Company No. 5, earning herself a permanent position as the patroness of local firefighters. She rode in countless parades, and even after growing out of riding on trucks, she supported the men in times of need. She married a successful stockbroker and traveled the world, becoming a person of note in the courts of Napoléon III and the maharaja of India. Coit left part of her fortune, more than $100,000, to beautify the city in an "appropriate manner." The city decided to use the funds to help pay tribute to San Francisco's firefighters in the form of Coit Tower. The unpainted reinforced concrete tower, designed in the Art Deco style, was dedicated in 1933. Murals decorate the interior, glorifying the integrity of working people. The murals were part of the Works Progress Administration's Federal Art Project, which helped artists get work during the Great Depression.

VIEW OF THE WATERFRONT FROM TELEGRAPH HILL

Telegraph Hill has the largest concentration of pre-1870s structures in the city

Above: This view from Telegraph Hill shows the San Francisco waterfront in the 1940s, bustling with wartime industry. When the gold rush created the instant city, new construction clustered on Telegraph Hill. During the fire of 1906, Telegraph Hill was mostly spared due to the efforts of residents who managed to divert the flames. The city's largest concentration of pre-1870 structures remains standing there today. The cliffs on the east side of the hill became steeper due to fifty years of quarrying. Ship captains used the rocky hillside to provide ballast for their ships; as the city grew, the rock was used to grade streets. Marchant Gardens is a city landmark named for one resident of the hill. Grace Marchant holds a legendary position among preservationists. She took a trash-strewn area near the Filbert Street Steps and converted it into a lush and varied urban garden, providing a habitat for many species of tropical and native birds, including the famed wild parrots of Telegraph Hill.

Right: Over the years, cargo handling on the San Francisco waterfront has largely faded. While some maritime uses continue on this stretch, much of the region's freight handling now occurs at the Port of Oakland across the bay. Ferries come in fewer numbers, and private vessels and cruise ships are more likely to ply these waters. One of the area's two large drydocks for repairing oversized vessels recently opened farther to the south at Hunter's Point, a location that once had several working navy facilities. The area pictured features several waterfront restaurants, where tourists and residents can relax in places that once boomed with industry. In later years, Telegraph Hill's commanding views and historic charm changed perceptions of the neighborhood from a detached throwback to a smart investment. Many developers have eyed the tiny cottages dating to the 1850s and envisioned forty stories of gold, but ardent neighborhood activism has protected these aged survivors.

COLUMBUS AVENUE

An intersection at the heart of San Francisco's Italian community

Above: Columbus Avenue intersects with Washington and Kearny streets to form a triangular parcel of real estate, or gore. Architects adapted to these gores by creating flatiron buildings, named for their resemblance to clothes irons. In 1927 the Jacopetti family opened a Nash automobile dealership in the flatiron building at 1 Columbus Avenue. The family no doubt sold cars using Nash's slogan, "Give the customer more than he has paid for." The Jacopettis had an impressive lineup to offer anyone who could afford to pay a whopping $1,000 for a car. In 1929 the Jacopetti dealership moved to 620 Washington Street.

Right: To better connect the Montgomery Block (on the site of today's Transamerica Pyramid) with the industrial area along the waterfront, a diagonal street called Montgomery Avenue was cut through North Beach in 1873 at a cost of $1.5 million. In 1909, to honor North Beach's predominantly Italian population and remember Christopher Columbus, the street's name was changed to Columbus Avenue. The intersection still lies at the heart of North Beach, which to every San Franciscan is synonymous with the Italian community that still calls the area home. An alleyway near where Columbus Avenue and Washington Street intersect bears the name of Jack Kerouac. The Beat writer lived there and visited another of San Francisco's many landmarks: the City Lights Bookstore at Columbus and Broadway. The Nash buildingis now home to Martha Egan's vintage clothes store.

BROADWAY

Broadway's hill was cut through to aid deliveries to and from Broadway Pier

Left: This 1860s photo shows the hill on Broadway between Montgomery and Kearney streets that made it tough on nineteenth-century horsepower. Broadway played an especially important role in San Francisco's early history. Teamsters used the street to deliver their wares to and from the Broadway Pier. Wealthy passengers arrived at the pier and expected a comfortable carriage ride from their steamships and ferries to Portsmouth Square at the heart of the city. As was the case with many of San Francisco's streets, Broadway had its steep hills. To solve the problems of getting people to "the Square" more efficiently and carrying wares to and from the pier at the foot of Broadway, they cut through the hill. Russian Hill, off in the distance, offered its own challenge. In 1863 Abner Doble, whose grandson and namesake later made steam automobiles, had planned to build a tunnel under the hill; his dream was not realized until December 21, 1952, when the Broadway Tunnel opened, taking traffic under Russian Hill.

Above: Cutting Broadway through between Kearney and Montgomery helped relieve nineteenth-century congestion, but the real challenge lay six blocks away at Russian Hill. On May 1, 1950, eighty-nine years after Abner Doble dreamed of cutting a tunnel under the hill, the Morrison-Knudsen Construction Company began work on the 1,616-foot-long Broadway Tunnel; the eleven-foot-wide twin bores extend from Powell to Larkin streets. The tunnel, whose gray superstructure intrudes onto the street across from the white-spired Our Lady of Guadalupe Church, officially opened on December 21, 1952. The Broadway Tunnel carries its namesake street under Russian Hill for three blocks. The east portal is located just past the Mason Street overpass; the west portal is just before the Hyde Street overpass. The tunnel brings the nineteenth-century dream of providing the flattest, most direct route from North Beach and Chinatown to Russian Hill, the Marina, and Pacific Heights.

BARBARY COAST

At one time the center of San Francisco's underworld

Left: The words "Barbary Coast" meant one thing in the nineteenth and early twentieth centuries: the district where one could enjoy the less-than-finer things of life. The dancing girl's leg on the Barbary Coast Theater's marquee hints at what awaits inside. The marquee promises a floor show, dining, dancing, and girls. One of the most unsavory theaters in early Barbary Coast days was the Bella Union. A firsthand description of a Bella Union performance was printed in the *San Francisco Call* in 1869: "Songs and dances of licentious and profane character while away the hours of the evening." That could describe any theater in the neighborhood. "When night lets fall its dusky curtain, the Coast brightens into life, and becomes the wild carnival of crime that has lain in lethargy during the sunny hours of the day," read the *Call*. A group of residents bent on vigilante justice, the Vigilante Committee, twice raided the Barbary Coast in an attempt to curtail the crime and vice in the days before the formation of the San Francisco Police Department.

Above: Today the former Barbary Coast is quieter, the bars and brothels are gone. Prior to the 1906 quake, the Coast was described as spanning the blocks along the shoreline between the Ferry Building and Fisherman's Wharf, including the slope of Telegraph Hill. The history of debauchery in the area was legendary. While men could be expected to rob, mug, shanghai, bribe, and beat, women in the Coast were also brutal. Besides the open prostitution, one fourteen-year-old girl ran her own gang, while a "Miss Piggott special" drink would knock out a sailor and send him off to Shanghai. After the 1906 quake, the Coast was reined in to just this single block of Pacific Street between Kearney and Montgomery streets. Today, the Coast is a sedate place of valuable property converted to modern uses.

SENTINEL BUILDING

Home to Francis Ford Coppola's American Zoetrope Studios since 1972

Left: Located in the heart of North Beach, the flatiron Sentinel Building's footprint stands on the triangle formed by Columbus Avenue and Jackson and Kearny streets. The building was under construction when the 1906 earthquake struck. It survived the temblor and dominated the scene on Columbus Avenue until its much-bigger brother appeared in the form of the Transamerica Pyramid just down the avenue at Montgomery Street. The Sentinel Building's top floor once housed Abe Ruef's political machine. Ruef founded the Union Labor Party and chose violin player and conductor Eugene Schmitz as a front for the party. Schmitz was elected mayor and served from 1902 to 1907 (he was known as "the Earthquake Mayor.") When a new owner took over in 1958, the building was renamed the Columbus Tower.

Above: The Sentinel Building's copper has gracefully aged, as its green patina lends the building its own personality. In the 1960s, the recording studio in the building was home to the Kingston Trio; the Grateful Dead recorded their song "Anthem in the Sun" in this studio. The building has been home to director Francis Ford Coppola's company American Zoetrope Studios since 1972. The company used the twelve-seat screening room in the basement to record Martin Sheen's voice-overs for the film *Apocalypse Now*. Over the years, the building has housed Enrico Banducci's restaurant, the Hungry I, while some say Caesar Cardini, who claims to have invented Caesar salad, had a restaurant here. Visitors can enjoy Italian cuisine and wine from Coppola's own Napa Valley vineyard in the Sentinel Building's Café Zoetrope.

CHINATOWN

The second most densely populated
neighborhood in the United States

This building at the intersection of Grant Avenue and
California Street lies at the heart of San Francisco's
Chinatown. The neighborhood, known as Chinatown
since the very early days of the city, adjoined the
Barbary Coast and lent its mystique to the era of
dives and dance halls, opium dens, and brothels.
Chinese laundries were rumored to hide secret
tunnels connecting opium dens and hideouts where
gangs serving the Chinese Consolidated Benevolent
Association (also known as the Six Companies) made
their plans to defend or attack the other ethnic gangs
and corner their markets of vice. In the decades
following the Emancipation Proclamation, forces of
temperance expressed concern over city aristocrats
and politicians making use of opium dens and the
fact that Chinese men still treated Chinese women
as slaves. Plenty of honest, hardworking men and
women of Chinese descent helped build the West,
providing hard labor for the transcontinental railroad,
marshland reclamation, and other giant public works
projects, all while many people of European descent
attempted to exclude them from society.

After the 1906 fire completely wiped out the neighborhood, Chinatown rose from the ashes along with the rest of the city. The Chinese solidified their place in California history and found racist and exclusionary practices against them slowly beginning to fade. Today people come from all over to enjoy the many Chinese restaurants here, like the one that occupies the ground floor of this building today. Dim sum—the delicacy smorgasbord Chinese lunch—and the originality of the many Chinatown shops draw many thousands of tourists to this neighborhood every year. Grant Avenue itself ranks as one of the most traveled tourist routes in town, as it provides an entertaining pedestrian route from Union Square to North Beach. San Francisco's Chinatown is the second most densely populated neighborhood in the United States, following New York's Chinatown.

MONTGOMERY BLOCK / TRANSAMERICA PYRAMID

The 1971 Transamerica Pyramid is
San Francisco's tallest building

It's hard to imagine that the four-story Montgomery Block (or "Monkey Block" as the locals called it in its waning years) was the tallest building in the West when it was built in 1853. Henry W. Halleck financed the building, and San Franciscans derided the structure as "Halleck's Folly." The building took up an entire city block and had two inner courts, salons, libraries, and billiards parlors. Two-foot-thick masonry walls and heavy iron shutters at every window helped protect against earthquake and fire damage. In fact, the Montgomery Block survived the 1868 earthquake and was the only large downtown building to survive the 1906 earthquake and the fire that followed on its heels. The Montgomery Block was demolished in 1959, and ten years later construction began on what many consider to be San Francisco's most recognizable building, the Transamerica Pyramid.

San Francisco's tallest building, the forty-eight-story Transamerica Pyramid—once home to the Transamerica Insurance Company— reaches 853 feet into the sky. Construction began in 1969, and the first tenants moved in three years later. Architect William Pereira designed the building's fifty-two-foot-deep steel-and-concrete foundation to move with earthquakes. The 6.9-magnitude Loma Prieta earthquake shook the building for more than a minute. The top story swayed almost a foot from side to side, but the building was undamaged. A 1,000-watt high-voltage red neon lamp, called an "aircraft light," flashes at the building's apex at night. In 1999 the building was acquired by the Dutch insurance company Aegon when it purchased the Transamerica Company. Aegon still markets Transamerica's insurance and uses the building as a logo.

NOB HILL

Showing the stately manors of Charles Crocker
and David Doughty Colton

Respected photographer Eadweard Muybridge set up a battery of
thirteen cameras in Mark Hopkins's mansion on Nob Hill in 1878. The
result was a seventeen-foot-long panorama of San Francisco. The pair
of panels shown here includes the stately manors belonging to Charles
Crocker and David Doughty Colton and a mound of earth that would later

be leveled to accommodate James Flood's mansion. Look closely at the
left panel and you'll notice a tall fence with the roof of a home peeking
out. Charles Crocker owned the palatial home next to the fence. The
railroad baron's next-door neighbor, an undertaker named Nicolas Yung,
refused to sell his property to Crocker. Crocker built a "spite fence" to
ruin Yung's view. Crocker hoped the fence would force the undertaker to
sell his property and move. Yung refused, and painted a skull and
crossbones on his roof to return the favor and to remind the Crocker
family that he was proud of his profession. On the far right can be seen
men working on the rails for the streetcar on today's Mason Street.

The firestorm that followed the 1906 earthquake leveled the mansions the Big Four called home. In 1926 the Mark Hopkins Hotel replaced Mark Hopkins's mansion. Architect Houghton Sawyer designed the building on the left in 1913 "in the French style" for the Morsehead family. Its bay windows accommodate the building's oval-shaped apartments. The twin-spired Grace Cathedral replaced Crocker's mansion and Huntington Park, across from the cathedral, recalls another member of the railroad's Big Four, Collis Huntington, who moved into Colton's handsome Italianate-style home in 1890. One mansion remains to remind us of Nob Hill's nabobs: the Flood

Mansion. James Flood was a member of another exclusive club whose members numbered four men. Silver barons Flood, William S. O'Brien, John W. Mackay, and James G. Fair controlled the precious ore that flowed from Nevada's Comstock Lode. Flood built a forty-two-room mansion with stone quarried in Connecticut, cut and dressed in New Jersey, and shipped around Cape Horn to San Francisco. After the temblor struck in 1906, fire destroyed Flood's home, but not beyond repair. The Pacific-Union Club bought the home in 1907. The men-only enclave still calls it home.

PANORAMA FROM NOB HILL

Taken from the Mark Hopkins mansion—now the site of the Mark Hopkins Hotel

Top: This panorama taken from Nob Hill in 1902 helps the viewer envision the city prior to the earthquake and fire of 1906. Several photographers used the roof of Mark Hopkins's Nob Hill mansion to capture the city by the bay. The main features of the hill in gold rush days were the mansions of the Big Four. Once the California Street cable car made the top of the hill accessible in the 1870s, railroad magnates Leland Stanford, Mark Hopkins, Collis Huntington, and Charles Crocker erected or bought mansions with commanding views of the wild, bustling shoreline. The Big Four would have preferred to look down their noses at places like the Barbary Coast. However, the tops of their mansions and of the silver barons' properties—James Flood's home and the Fairmont Hotel that James Fair's daughters built—offered some incredible places to take in the growing metropolis. Every one of these suffered damage in the earthquake and ensuing fire; only the Flood mansion and the Fairmont Hotel remained standing.

Bottom: The Big Four colored Nob Hill as we know it today. The "four associates," as they preferred to be called, co-owned the Central Pacific Railroad (CPRR) that would serve as the western end of the first transcontinental line. CPRR president Leland Stanford, later the founder of Stanford University, had a Nob Hill mansion that burned in the 1906 fire. The granite wall surrounding the mansion's grounds serves today as part of the Stanford Court Hotel. CPRR vice president Collis Huntington constantly vied with Stanford for control of various holdings the two shared. In 1890 Huntington purchased David Douty Colton's mansion. The site of CPRR treasurer Mark Hopkins's mansion, an incredible Queen Anne–style palace with multiple towers that burned in the fire, became the site of the opulent nineteen-story InterContinental Mark Hopkins Hotel. Charles Crocker, who served as CPRR's construction supervisor, had a mansion at the site of today's Grace Cathedral.

FORT GUNNYBAGS

Residents took the law into their own hands here

Fort Gunnybags, home to the Vigilante Committee, was located in the wholesale liquor house of Truett and Jones on Sacramento Street, about a block from the waterfront. The fort took its name from bags made of gunny cloth—a strong, coarse material made from jute. To protect the fort, committee members filled the bags with sand and piled them against the wall. The fort was the scene of meetings, mock trials, and hangings. The bell in the photograph hangs in the Society of California Pioneers' library today. The 1906 earthquake and fire destroyed the original bronze tablet placed in 1903. The Native Sons of the Golden West replaced that plaque in a ceremony on June 1, 1918. The plaque was removed during construction of Bethlehem Steel's headquarters at the site and rededicated in 1960. The inset photo shows members of the Native Sons at the plaque's rededication on December 16, 1960.

The site of Fort Gunnybags stands in the shadow of the Embarcadero in today's Financial District, a business hub that corporations, law firms, and banks call home. Visa, Wells Fargo, the Charles Schwab Corporation, McKesson Corporation, and Barclays Global Investors are just a few of the business giants with roots in the district. Seventy-five years before the advent of the Financial District, Fort Gunnybags took up the entire block bounded by California, Front, Battery, and Sacramento streets. It's easy to miss the plaque on the seven-story building with the red facade at 275 Sacramento Street. This building's footprint takes up the entrance to the fort, which was actually at 243 Sacramento Street, in a building that was part of the Classic Revival–style warehouse known as the Sacramento Block. The 1906 earthquake destroyed the entire block.

SAN FRANCISCO PANORAMA

A classic view of San Francisco with fog barreling in over the Golden Gate Bridge

In May 1949, *San Francisco News-Call Bulletin* photographer Bob Warren snapped this panoramic photograph that shows the fog rolling over the Golden Gate Bridge. "Cooling fog came creeping into the Golden Gate early today to bring relief to the sweltering city and end a two-day hot spell that set records for this time of the year," said the caption that accompanied the photograph in the May 7 *News-Call Bulletin* editions. Warren's photograph took in the Palace of Fine Arts, the Marina District, Cow Hollow, and the slopes of Pacific Heights, where he set up his camera at Pacific Avenue and Fillmore Street. Freshwater springs once formed a lagoon in an area known as Spring Valley. The neighborhood's dairy farmers decided that the name Cow Hollow better described the landscape; the name stuck. The Marina District sprung up in the wake of the 1915 Panama-Pacific International Exposition that added the Palace of Fine Arts to the setting.

The view from Pacific Avenue and Fillmore Street has changed little since 1949. This photograph without the fog offers a sharper view of the Marin Headlands across the bay from San Francisco. This look at the headlands, which are a part of the Golden Gate National Recreation Area, includes Hawk Hill to the right of the southern (left) span of the Golden Gate Bridge, Kirby Cove between the spans, Battery Spencer near the bridge's northern span, and Lime Point at the span's base. A section of the Pacific Coast Range can be seen in the distance, with 2,571-foot Mount Tamalpais rising up on the right. Each year from August into December, the 920-foot Hawk Hill serves as a lookout point to observe the migration of falcons, eagles, and the eponymous hawks. The lighthouse at Lime Point dates back to an 1833 fog-signal station. San Francisco may be home to the "crookedest street," but until 1931 Mount Tamalpais boasted the "crookedest railroad in the world."

CLAY STREET TO NOB HILL

Andrew Hallidie's cable car operated
here from 1873 to 1942

Left: Few remember that a cable car once climbed Clay
Street from Kearny Street to Nob Hill, but many know
the name of the inventor who made it possible—Andrew
Hallidie. Hallidie began working on the concept of a
cable-car line in 1869. He had seen horsecar employees
whipping their animals as they struggled up Jackson
Street on the wet cobblestones. Thanks to Hallidie's
invention of the cable grip, the Clay Street Hill Railroad,
the world's first cable-car line, began carrying passengers
on September 1, 1873—the same year this photo was
taken. At first the line just took riders to Mason Street,
then to Leavenworth Street. In 1877 the company extended
the line to Van Ness Avenue. That same year, competition
made things interesting when the California Street
Railroad started construction on a cable line just one
block over. The line began carrying passengers on April
10, 1878, up California Street from Kearny to Fillmore.

Right: Andrew Hallidie's Clay Street Hill Railroad fared
well despite competition from the California Railroad.
Hallidie's cable cars ran up and down Clay Street from
1873 until 1942, when the Market Street Railway stepped
in and converted the cable-car line to a trolleybus
operation. The idea of a trolleybus is almost as old as
that of the cable car. It dates back to 1882, when Dr.
Ernst Werner von Siemens ran a trolleybus he called the
Elektromote in a Berlin suburb. A trolleybus draws its
power from a network of charged overhead wires. One
of these buses traverses much of the same route today
as the Clay Street Hill Railroad did in the past (albeit one-
way, as Clay Street now runs in just one direction down
from Nob Hill). Today the 1 California line does the honors.

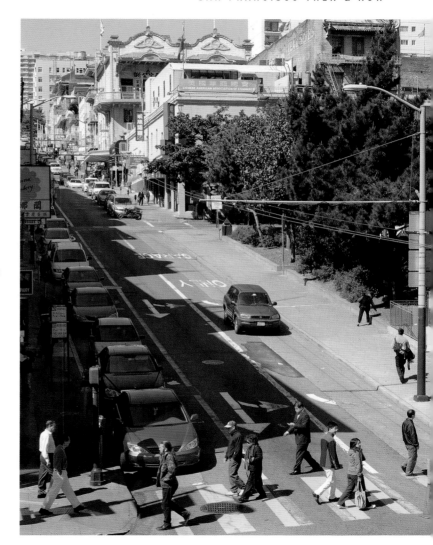

PARROTT BUILDING / FINANCIAL DISTRICT

John Parrott's San Francisco Savings Union was the first stone building in the city

Left: The first stone building in San Francisco went up on the corner of Montgomery and California streets. The Parrott Building (named for John Parrott, who financed the venture) was built with stone from China. Parrott had to hire Chinese laborers to construct the building because no one else could read the Chinese mason marks on the stone. At first the Chinese masons refused to start working, as they claimed that the location of the building went against the principles of feng shui. Eventually the importer and banker must have made it worth their while to compromise their beliefs, for the building was completed in 1852. It survived the 1906 earthquake, convincing many of the wisdom of building with masonry. The San Francisco Savings Union, Parrott's company, opened its doors again for business soon after the fire went out. In the foreground, a streetcar offers rides to the Willows, a resort near today's Eighteenth and Valencia streets.

Above: In 1926 the Parrott Building was razed and replaced with the Financial Center Building, putting to good use the site at the heart of the Financial District. While no quaint streetcar offers to take riders to bucolic resorts in the Mission neighborhood, one can now catch a Bay Area Rapid Transit (BART) railcar, a cab, or a bus. The concept of the Willows, a quiet retreat in today's busy urban Mission neighborhood, is an amusing contrast. The city has long since encompassed the area southeast of Mission Dolores known for its stand of willows and chaparral serenely receding into the distance. Today, one can eat at some of the finest taquerias in the Bay Area there. Mission Street taquerias stay true to Mexican traditions, serving irresistible tacos, enchiladas, and plenty more Mexican fare. The area has also earned a reputation for breeding talent in the visual arts. Many Mission-area artists have contributed to their neighborhood with striking, colorful murals.

PORTSMOUTH SQUARE

Named for Commander John B. Portsmouth, who arrived here in 1846

Left: California's first- and second-generation settlers from Mexico broke their bonds with their homeland, calling themselves "Californios." The plaza of the pueblo they named Yerba Buena stood on the site of today's Portsmouth Square. On July 6, 1846, Commander John B. Portsmouth sailed into San Francisco Bay, anchored in Yerba Buena Cove, and came ashore to raise the American flag and claim Yerba Buena for the United States. Soon the square bore the name of his flagship. After that, gold rush settlers transformed the square into a beautifully landscaped urban retreat. A destitute Robert Louis Stevenson whiled away his time here in 1879 until his father sent him enough money to live on. A marker commemorating the presence of the author of *Treasure Island* can be found on the square today.

Above: In 1962 the construction of a four-level underground parking garage converted the square to what many consider the garage's "roof garden." Portsmouth Square fell into disrepair and disuse until the city started paying attention in the late 1980s. Since then, the square has experienced a series of renovations, at a cost of $3.9 million. The facelift included elevators, a playground, tables for Chinese chess, benches, and landscaping. After experiencing fifteen years as an urban renewal project on top of a parking garage that accommodates more than 50,000 vehicles a month, a fresh, new Portsmouth Square made its public debut in 2001. Portsmouth Square is today a part of Chinatown; many consider the square its heart. The *Goddess of Democracy* statue, a gift from the San Francisco Goddess of Democracy Statue Project to the city, helps cement this identity.

SACRAMENTO STREET LOOKING WEST FROM MONTGOMERY

Now at the center of the Financial District commute

Left: This 1860s view is of Sacramento Street looking west from Montgomery. This and the photograph on page 68 show a several-block-long stretch of Sacramento Street on the same day. Photographers from the San Francisco firm Lawrence and Houseworth set up their cameras, first looking one direction and then the other, to create these incidental pictures that capture a moment in time. In this photograph, looking west, we can take in the *Alta California* newspaper's headquarters and what looks to be a Nob Hill mansion under construction in the distance. Montgomery Street was named for Captain John B. Montgomery, who claimed San Francisco for the United States during the Mexican War.

Above: Today, standing at the corner of Sacramento and Montgomery streets on weekday mornings puts one directly in the path of the Financial District pedestrian commute. After 5:00 p.m. a similar herd can be seen moving south on Montgomery, heading for the BART station and home in any number of outlying communities. Sacramento Street looking west shows how taller buildings now obscure the contour of Nob Hill, but multistory buildings in the distance show the location of luxury hotels and apartments. Sacramento Street was originally named Howard Street for William D. Howard, a true public servant and early city councilman. A street south of Market now bears the name Howard.

SACRAMENTO STREET LOOKING
EAST FROM MONTGOMERY

This area now contains some of the tallest buildings in downtown

Left: This 1860s view of Sacramento Street, looking east from Montgomery toward the bay, was taken on the same day as the image on page 66. A stationer has set up shop on the corner opposite the newspaper, a good location because reporters were likely their steady customers. Photographers, like those of Lawrence and Houseworth who took this image, found themselves developing their new medium along with the growth of the city. Lawrence and Houseworth were among the most important early firms, established in 1852. For about forty years, the firm's employees photographed the city as it grew. Their work served as the basis of the firm's three-volume collection of nearly 1,500 images that customers chose from when ordering a print. The collection is preserved today thanks to the work of the Society of California Pioneers.

Above: In today's view, automobiles have replaced wagons and the stationer's has become an office tower. Further down the street, all the buildings have risen up, as this area contains some of the tallest buildings in the downtown area. The corner of Montgomery and Sacramento was the site of another historic photograph. Famed portrait photographer Arnold Genthe rushed to his camera dealer at Montgomery and Sacramento on a particular morning in 1906 because all of his equipment had been ruined by falling plaster. The dealer told the photographer, "Take anything you want, this place is going to burn up anyway." Genthe walked up Sacramento Street a few blocks and immediately captured the attitude of the people on the street looking east toward the bay. A large cloud of smoke loomed over the buildings in the distance.

FERRY BUILDING

The Central Pacific Railroad built the first one in 1877 for $93,000

Left: In this circa-1879 photograph, horsecars await passengers in front of the Union Depot and Ferry House. The Central Pacific Railroad built the Ferry House at the foot of Market Street in 1877 for $93,000. The 350-foot-long building stretched from Clay Street to Market Street with four boat slips—two reserved exclusively for the railroad's ferries. Prior to the building's appearance on the waterfront, passengers used a much smaller wharf at Davis Street. To handle increasing traffic, the Central Pacific later extended the structure 250 feet south in order to add three more slips. The terminal now had seven slips: four for ferry traffic from Oakland, one for Alameda, and two from Marin County and the North Coast. In 1883 the Market Street Cable Railroad began operations. Today's Ferry Building replaced it in 1898 to handle increased traffic.

Above: On November 8, 1891, California voters approved the San Francisco Ferry Depot Act by the slimmest of margins: around 180,000 men went to the polls (women couldn't vote until 1920) and the bond measure passed by just 866 votes. Architect A. Page Brown had already submitted his plans to the Port Commission; work began in January 1893. For the plain structure atop the Union Depot and Ferry House that his building would replace, Brown substituted an elegant 240-foot-high tower. He took his inspiration for the tower from La Giralda, the twelfth-century minaret that the Moors built in Seville, Spain, now used as a bell on the city's cathedral. Brown's masterpiece underwent a meticulous restoration in 2004. The 600-foot-long passenger concourse was opened up through the removal of 1950s office space. Large openings were cut into the second floor to allow more light to reach the ground level. Using European arcades and department stores as models, designers left room for the local artisans and restaurants that call the Ferry Building home today.

VIEW FROM THE FERRY BUILDING

Showing the devastation left by the 1906 earthquake

Left: This striking view from the Ferry Building after the earthquake and fire of 1906 shows only one habitable structure: a tent at the lower right of the photograph. The fact that the streetcars are running along Market Street so soon after the temblor shows the resilience that will quickly rebuild the city. One bright side of the city's reconstruction was that jobs were suddenly plentiful; not enough labor could be found. Military cadets from the University of California–Berkeley were temporarily committed as a labor unit to San Francisco and earned the city's respect while fighting the fire or defending homes from looters. Cities around the region committed themselves to rebuilding the fallen city by sending firefighters, construction material, and other supplies by rail and ferry. Many citizens opened their homes to the hundreds of thousands of sudden refugees. Tent cities appeared both in town and in other Bay Area communities. Just after the disaster, hundreds of displaced dogs and cats wandered the city, lost in a place they no longer recognized.

Above: The view from the Ferry Building tower today is a heartening view of urban life at its finest. The San Franciscans below enjoy tremendous opportunity and prosperity. Along Market Street, a wide diversity of stores lure customers. Cultural experiences abound in any number of theaters, galleries, museums, boutiques, and bars, all within a few blocks' walk. Innovation and entrepreneurship have always been part of San Francisco's economy, and job creation continues in information technology, biotech, and health care. On the Embarcadero Plaza below, artisans and craftspeople gather in a bazaar on a regular basis. In the shadow of the tower, one of the area's finest farmer's markets brings shoppers from around the Bay Area each Sunday. Gone are the streetcars on Market Street, but the Ferry Building still greets ferries, buses, and light-rail. The MUNI line, which runs past the Ferry Building on Embarcadero, uses streetcars that have been recycled from other cities, including Philadelphia and Oporto, Portugal.

BAY BRIDGE

Built between 1933 and 1936 to link San Francisco with Oakland

Left: Workers hewed a tunnel through the heart of Yerba Buena Island to support the roadbed that allowed traffic to flow across the Bay Bridge (officially named the San Francisco–Oakland Bay Bridge). This was not the first time a bridge from Oakland to San Francisco had been on the drawing board. In 1869 the Central Pacific Railroad hoped to take over Yerba Buena Island for a bridge from Oakland's Long Wharf into San Francisco. The idea of taking over Goat Island (as locals called Yerba Buena) for private enterprise got the federal government on its heels; troops were sent in. The caper went down in history as the "Goat Island Grab." Today the island anchors the bridge; a suspension bridge takes drivers into San Francisco, while a more complicated system consisting of a double-tower cantilever span, five medium-span truss bridges, and a fourteen-section truss causeway on the other side of the tunnel leads into Oakland.

Above: The upper deck of the Bay Bridge's suspension span takes drivers from Yerba Buena Island onto Rincon Hill and into San Francisco, while the lower deck carries traffic into the East Bay. The Bay Bridge seldom gets as much attention as San Francisco Bay's other suspension bridge, the Golden Gate Bridge. When the Bay Bridge first opened in 1936, the bridge's upper deck carried three lanes of automobile traffic in each direction. Automobiles on the lower deck shared the road with trucks, trains, and streetcars. Two railroad tracks were built on the south side of the lower deck for the electric commuter trains of the Southern Pacific, the Key System, and the Sacramento Northern Rail Service.

PALACE HOTEL

The hotel was completely rebuilt following the earthquake of 1906

How many diners in the Palace Hotel's Garden Court know that they are enjoying their meals where horse-driven cabs once deposited their wealthy passengers? When the Palace Hotel opened in 1875, the Palace Court served as the hotel's carriage entrance. The hotel's hydraulic elevators, or "rising rooms," caused guests to marvel at the convenience. Each room had air-conditioning and a call button so guests could put in requests to the concierge. Both of these images show the hotel in its pre-1906 glory. Three years of reconstruction followed the earthquake and fire of 1906. Artist Maxfield Parrish was commissioned to paint a sixteen-foot mural in the new Pied Piper Bar. The hotel again rose to prominence, welcoming dignitaries such as U.S. presidents Harrison, McKinley, Grant, Taft, Harding, Wilson, Clinton, and both Roosevelts. In 1945 the Palace Hotel hosted a banquet in honor of the first session of the United Nations.

When the Palace Hotel reopened in 1909, the carriage entrance was transformed into the Garden Court, which had a domed stained-glass ceiling and Austrian crystal chandeliers. The hotel was completely refurbished in 1991 and today it features 553 guest rooms with fourteen-foot ceilings, just like it did back in 1909. The Palace Hotel offers the absolute finest in accommodations to all its guests. The restaurant choices in the hotel are legendary. Parrish's *The Pied Piper of Hamelin* mural still graces the Pied Piper Bar, which was named one of the top bars in the world by *Esquire* magazine. Maxfield's offers warm parlor-style dining, and Kyo-ya celebrates San Francisco's long love affair with Japanese cuisine. The Garden Court's incredibly opulent ceiling gives diners the sense of feasting in a European palace.

CHRONICLE BUILDING

Showing preparations for the Knights of Pythias parade of 1902

Left: The Chronicle Building's clock tower provides the background for workers balancing themselves above Market and Kearny streets as they prepare lights for the Knights of Pythias parade on August 13, 1902. Justus H. Rathbone founded the Order of Knights of Pythias in 1864 as an international fraternity. The Knights met in the Palace Hotel, just down the street from where the workers were stringing the lights. The inset photo shows these festive lights adorning Market Street and covering the Call Building—home to the *San Francisco Call* newspaper—across from the Chronicle Building, which Chicago architects Daniel Burnham and John Root designed to house Michael Henry de Young's newspaper empire in 1890. San Francisco's newspaper industry was once concentrated in one spot with the juxtaposition of the Chronicle, Call, and Examiner buildings at Market and Third streets.

Above: The festive lights and the Chronicle Building's clock tower disappeared long ago—the lights were dismantled shortly after the Knights of Pythias left town, and the clock tower was leveled less than four years later by the 1906 earthquake and fire. The bronze clock didn't even last that long. In 1905 supporters of the newly reelected mayor, Eugene Schmitz, whom the *Chronicle* had opposed, set the clock on fire with rockets fired from the street. After the temblor, Willis Polk, who ran Burnham and Root's San Francisco office, rebuilt the structure with office space in place of the clock tower. The *Chronicle* left the building for more spacious digs on Mission Street in 1924. During a 1962 remodel, enameled metal porcelain stripped the building of its nineteenth-century personality. The building is now home to the Ritz-Carlton Club, which offers private residences with resort-style amenities.

LOTTA'S FOUNTAIN

Named for entertainer Lotta Crabtree,
"the San Francisco Favorite"

Entertainer Lotta Crabtree began her career dancing, singing, and playing banjo among rugged mining camps of California and Nevada. After moving to San Francisco in 1856, it took Lotta just three years to attain the nickname "Miss Lotta, the San Francisco Favorite." While Lotta had the performing talent, her mother Mary Ann had a talent for artist management. The elder Crabtree followed her daughter, sweeping up gold nuggets and dust that adoring miners threw onto the stage. Mary Ann filled a leather bag with these sweepings; as the years ensued, the bag became heavier. After seven years of gathering more notoriety, Mary Ann turned the gold in the bag into local real estate. Miss Lotta went east and garnered more fame and fortune acting in plays there. By 1875 the bag, now a steamer trunk, had grown too heavy again, and Mary Ann bought a twenty-two-room cottage in New Jersey. Lotta then financed her own national touring company and gave San Francisco a fountain.

The Crabtrees carried on a campaign of donating fountains to cities they visited. Lotta's Fountain still stands at the intersection of Market, Geary, and Kearny streets and serves as a meeting place every April 18 at 5:12 a.m. to remember the earthquake and fire of 1906. Immediately following the disaster, the fountain, one of the few landmarks left standing on Market Street, became a gathering point for survivors. A community bulletin board grew on the fountain, listing the names of people seeking lost friends, family, and associates, deceased or otherwise. Until 1905 when she passed on, Mary Ann kept turning extra income into real estate around the nation. After Mary Ann died, Miss Lotta retired to Boston and returned to San Francisco only once more: for Lotta Crabtree Day during the Panama-Pacific Exposition of 1915. She died in 1924 and left a $4 million fortune to charities benefiting animals, aging actors, and war veterans. The fountain underwent a restoration in 1974, during which it was moved about ten feet.

Sculptor Douglas Tilden completed The Mechanics, also called the Donahue Monument, in 1899; it was dedicated two years later on May 15, 1901, five years before the earthquake. This photograph with a man dejectedly reading the newspaper shows that the monument, like Lotta's Fountain, survived the temblor. James Mervyn Donahue commissioned Tilden, who was deaf, to create the monument in memory of Donahue's father, Peter. In 1849 Peter, Michael, and James Donahue opened a blacksmith's shop at First and Mission streets, which later expanded into the foundry that became the Union Iron Works. Tilden, who has been called "San Francisco's Father of Sculpture," also created Admission Day at Market and Post streets, California Volunteers at Mission and Delores streets, and The Baseball Player in Golden Gate Park.

MECHANICS MONUMENT

A source of inspiration in the rebuilding of the city following the 1906 earthquake

The monument was a source of inspiration in the rebuilding of San Francisco following the 1906 earthquake. The ten-ton statue, which stands near the intersection of Bush, Battery, and Market streets, shows four ironworkers punching rivet holes in a piece of ship plate. The fountain is inscribed with the motto Labor omnia vincit ("Work conquers all"). A sidewalk plaque next to the monument marks the 1848 San Francisco Bay shoreline from Howard Street to Pacific Avenue. Tilden was born in 1860 and died in 1935. He was born hearing, but became deaf after contracting scarlet fever at the age of five. As involved as Tilden was in his calling as a sculptor, he found time to become deeply involved in the deaf community. He served as vice president of the World Federation of the Deaf and as president of the California Association of the Deaf.

The banner reads:

THE UNION The WHOLE UNION
& NOTHING BUT THE UNION.
WEBSTER.

LIBERTY and UNION now and Forever
ONE AND INSEPARABLE.
WEBSTER.

UNION RALLY OF 1861

Where Thomas Starr King's oratory "saved California for the Union"

Left: The Civil War began on April 12, 1861, but word did not reach California until early May. This May 1861 image shows a crowd at Market and Post streets listening to Thomas Starr King's rallying cries. King knew from an early age that he wanted to preach like his father, and he found success in Massachusetts in the 1850s. King had the power to help explain complex ideas to those who listened. He went west and attempted to further the cause of the Unitarian Church in wild San Francisco. King, like every American, had to choose a side in the conflict. He campaigned for the election of Abraham Lincoln, and in 1861 he began a campaign with three speeches to garner support for the Union. His efforts helped emplace a pro-Union state legislature. General Winfield Scott, commander in chief of the Union army, said King's oratory "saved California for the Union." The inset photo shows the Crocker Building in the 1930s at the same spot as the Union rally. This eleven-story flatiron building at Market and Post streets was completed in 1891.

Above: The Crocker Building survived the earthquake of 1906, only to be torn down in 1966 to make way for the Aetna office tower that opened in 1969. The late 1960s and 1970s brought increasingly taller buildings to San Francisco, as the office tower became the status symbol of the era. The Bank of America Center (now known as 555 California Street) also opened in 1969, at a height of 779 feet. This, along with 44 Market Street (565 feet), served as the first chapter of a time some called "the Manhattanization of San Francisco." These impressive office towers were soon joined by One Embarcadero Center (569 feet) in 1971 and the Transamerica Pyramid (853 feet) in 1972. The Pyramid replaced all others as the most distinctive building on the skyline, and remains the tallest in town. The proposed new Transbay Terminal redevelopment project includes a plan for ten new skyscrapers more than 400 feet tall, three of which will exceed 1,000 feet and become the city's tallest buildings. A. Page Brown, who designed today's Ferry Building, also designed this building, San Francisco's second skyscraper.

Market Street swarms with people celebrating the end of World War II on September 1, 1945; none of them seem to be paying attention to the fact that Abbott and Costello are playing in The Naughty Nineties at the Esquire Theatre. President Harry S. Truman had just announced that the Japanese surrendered and would be signing a peace accord the following day aboard the USS Missouri. Notice the word "Go" on the traffic signal. "You can see how much chance there was of autos going any place," someone wrote on the back of this photograph. The two buildings on the right side of the photograph, on either side of Fifth Street, housed the Hale Brothers Department Store. The tower of the Humboldt Bank Building stands farther down Market Street at Fourth Street.

MARKET STREET

Celebrating the end of World War II

Of the Hale Brothers Department Store, the Humboldt Bank Building, and the Esquire Theatre, only the Esquire is gone. It fell in 1972 to the wrecking ball when planners made way for the Powell Street BART station. Today, Hallidie Plaza stands in its place. The Esquire had almost as many lives as a cat. It opened in 1909 as the Market Street Theatre, one of the first large theaters on Market Street. It became the Alhambra in 1917, the Frolic in 1919, the Cameo in 1923, the Marion Davies in 1929, and finally the Esquire in 1940. During the war years it was a popular first-run outlet for Universal Studios' Abbott and Costello comedies as well as horror films. The Humboldt Bank Building survives with a new name, 875 Market Street, and the handsome Hale Brothers Department Store is now called 901 Market Street. The part of the Hale Brothers store that was once across Fifth Street is now part of the Westfield San Francisco Centre.

GRANT AVENUE AT O'FARRELL STREET

Documenting the destruction caused by the 1906 earthquake

Left: A driver and passenger aboard a vintage automobile pose with a photographer among the post-1906 earthquake ruins on Grant Avenue. The devastation left few reminders of what stood here just days before the earthquake. Seen in the photograph is one of the few commercial buildings that survived the temblor: the Shreve and Company Building at Grant Avenue and Post Street. The photographer set up his tripod at O'Farrell Street, a short block up from Market Street, to capture what little remained of this busy street that was named for Civil War hero and U.S. president Ulysses S. Grant. The street had two other names. When the Spanish laid it out in 1835, they called it Calle de Fundacion. After the mericans arrived, the street was renamed Dupont Street for Samuel Dupont, a captain aboard the USS ortsmouth. In 1876 the stretch of Dupont from Market to Bush Street was renamed for Grant; after the 1906 earthquake, the entire stretch was named for Grant.

Above: In order to get the Shreve and Company Building in the picture, a modern-day photographer has to move the camera two blocks up Grant Avenue from O'Farrell to Geary Street. The gray-tone Shreve and Company Building stands neatly tucked across Post Street from the nearly identical off-white affair that most San Franciscans fondly call "the Brooks Brothers Building." The Shreve and Company Building was built in 1905 and survived the 1906 earthquake, which left the property across Post Street in shambles. In 1909 an eleven-story building that seems to mimic Shreve's rose from the ashes. The clothier Brooks Brothers occupied the building's ground floor for some forty years. After a renovation honored by the American Association of Architects, the building has a new ground-floor tenant, the Italian luxury retailer Prada. Business continues to thrive across the street at Shreve and Company just as it has since they moved into their Post Street digs a month before the 1906 earthquake.

POWELL STREET

The 1906 earthquake destroyed almost everything seen in this 1896 photo

Left: A San Francisco News photographer took this picture of Powell and Sutter streets; it appeared in the newspaper on June 11, 1896, as part of its panorama series. A Powell Street cable car descends from Nob Hill, where the Leland Stanford mansion (on the right) and Mark Hopkins's home scrape the skyline. The Ferries and Cliff House Railway began running cable cars up and down Powell Street in 1888. In 1893 the Market Street Railway Company absorbed the line. The company painted its streetcars different colors: Powell-Mason cars were yellow and Powell-Jackson cars were green. The Powell Street car is yielding to two Sutter Street Railway cable cars with their grip cars and trailers; a teamster waits his turn with a horse and wagon. The line that once plied Sutter Street began service in 1863 as a horsecar line; it made the switch to cable in 1877. Ten years after this photograph appeared in the newspaper, the 1906 earthquake destroyed nearly everything seen here.

Above: In 1914 architect Frederick Meyer's nine-story Baroque-Renaissance building rose up on the northwest corner of Powell and Sutter. San Franciscans call it "500 Sutter" after its address. The American flag in the distance waves from atop the Mark Hopkins Hotel, which replaced the Hopkins mansion in 1926. The hotel was designed by the architectural firm of Weeks and Day. The cream-colored building with all those windows next door to the Hopkins is the newly renovated Renaissance Stanford Court. Built in 1912 as a luxury apartment house, it was gutted and rebuilt as a hotel in 1971. The redbrick building halfway up the hill houses "the Family," a club that was started in 1901 by newspapermen who were unable to get into the more prestigious Bohemian Club. Cable cars still ply Powell Street; the earthquake halted service until January 1907. United Railroads of San Francisco took over the Sutter Street Railway in 1902. After the earthquake, the line was electrified, and in 1945 it became a bus route.

Left: The cable-car turnaround at Powell and Market streets looks much the same today as it did in this 1940s photograph. The turnaround is located just a few blocks away from Union Square. The cable cars here carry passengers over the Powell Street hill to California Street and on to the Hyde Street Pier. But around the time of this photograph, the cable car's future was in jeopardy. Progress determined that the future belonged to the combustion engine, and soon streetcars, cable cars, and their tracks were pulled out of San Francisco and countless other cities nationwide. Some of these materials supported war efforts. The 1903 street railway directory listed schedules for cable-car lines named for the main streets they served: California (all the way to the Presidio); O'Farrell, Jones, and Hyde; Geary; Union; Castro; Haight; Hayes; Jackson; McAllister; Polk and Larkin; Powell-Mason; and Sutter and Valencia. Abbreviated versions of these lines exist today. The Powell-Mason, Powell-Hyde, and California lines continue to serve tourists and commuters alike, much to everyone's delight.

POWELL STREET TURNAROUND

Cable cars are turned 180 degrees for their next trip up Powell Street

Above: Of the many memorable locations along the cable-car lines, the Powell Street turnaround is where the cable cars "perform." Here tourists and spectators watch the gripman physically turn the cable car 180 degrees so it can continue in the opposite direction. It just so happens they pull this maneuver right where the civic center, theater district, shopping district, and a transit station all come together. On March 5, 2009, San Franciscan Herbie Hatman declared the great San Francisco Pie Fight underway at the Powell Street turnaround beginning at 5:39 p.m., just in time to shock tourists and commuters heading home. Formal attire was requested, however, resulting in a humorous spectacle.

PANORAMA FROM THE ST. FRANCIS HOTEL

Showing the fire that followed the 1906 earthquake

Above: This panorama may have been taken by Arthur C. Pillsbury, the inventor of the circuit panoramic camera. We do know that a photographer from the Pillsbury Picture Company stood atop the St. Francis Hotel on Union Square to take this remarkable gelatin silver print of the fire that followed on the heels of the earthquake on April 18, 1906. The statue of Victory gracing the top of sculptor Robert Aitkens's monument honoring naval hero Admiral George Dewey peeks from the bottom of the photograph, on the left. Fire has spared the buildings surrounding Union Square. The tall steel-frame structure near the square is the Whittell Building, then under construction; it still stands on Geary Street. The building under construction across the street is the Butler Building, which would later house the City of Paris Department Store. The Call Building's tower rises up behind the Butler Building, with the Mutual Savings Bank Building to its left.

Right: Victory still crowns the Dewey Monument at Union Square. The St. Francis Hotel survived the 1906 earthquake and still welcomes visitors from around the world, but much has changed since the Pillsbury Picture Company set up its camera on the hotel's roof on April 18, 1906. BART trains now roll beneath Market Street and the automobile, a rich man's toy at the time of the 1906 earthquake, brought about change, including a parking garage below historic Union Square. The Call Building still stands, and is today called the Central Tower. Albert Roller radically changed the building, however. He considered the building's handsome dome "uneconomical" and demolished it in 1937. Roller used the space to add six more stories to the building.

UNION SQUARE

Robert Aitkens's monument of Admiral Dewey is still the centerpiece of the square

Left: Union Square first came into existence after Jasper O'Farrell had completed the initial design for the city of San Francisco in 1847. O'Farrell defined Union Square and Washington Square as lands to be used for open space, but it wasn't until Colonel John Geary, San Francisco's first American mayor, deeded the land to the public closer to the eve of the Civil War that the park received its dedication. The site took on the name Union Square when it was used as the rallying point for those who hoped to preserve the Union and supported the North. By the 1880s, the area had grown into one of the city's finest residential neighborhoods, with three churches fronting on the square. In the early 1900s, commercial uses slowly squeezed out residences. The Dewey Monument is the centerpiece of the square. Erected in 1901, the column honored Admiral George Dewey for his naval victory during the Spanish-American War. A statue of the Roman goddess Victory stands atop the monument.

Above: Union Square today is synonymous with department stores, lavish boutiques, galleries, and cutting-edge electronics. But by the time the automobile had taken over in the 1930s, merchants, who now commanded the square, feared they would lose their businesses if the district could not find a way to offer ample parking for their customers. So began a campaign to construct the city's first underground parking garage. The only problem was the definition of ownership of the land beneath the square. If the public owned the surface of the land, could the city lease the ground underneath to a private company? This question went all the way to the California Supreme Court, and when the answer came back, it was yes. In 1941 the city broke ground on the parking garage that still exists under the square today. The square underwent another transformation and renovation in 1997, which was completed in 2002.

GOLDEN GATE THEATRE

"The official site of Broadway in San Francisco"

The limelight began to shine on vaudeville actors at the Golden Gate Theatre on March 26, 1922. G. Albert Lansburgh designed both the 2,844-seat Golden Gate Theatre (a movie theater) and the Warfield Building, which had its own famed vaudeville and movie theater, across Taylor Street. While attending the University of California–Berkeley, Lansburgh worked for architects Bernard Maybeck and Julius E. Krafft. After graduating, he moved to Paris and studied at the École des Beaux-Arts, earning his diploma in 1906. He returned to San Francisco just one month after the earthquake.

Today's Golden Gate Theatre bills itself as the "official site of Broadway in San Francisco" and lures theater fans from all over the West. The Golden Gate was converted into a two-screen theater in the 1960s. In 1979 the Shorenstein Hayes Nederlander Group restored the building to its original size and opened it as a performing arts center. Workers removed ten tons of steel (including an escalator), four tons of plaster, sheet rock, studs, insulation, and 4,000 square feet of plywood. The Golden Gate Theatre has hosted showstopping musicals like *A Chorus Line*, which reopened the theater on December 27, 1979. Richard Burton starred here in *Camelot*, Rex Harrison in *My Fair Lady*, and Topol in *Fiddler on the Roof*. The tradition continues today with Broadway hits like *Spamalot*, *Wicked*, and *Rent*—the film version was shot just around the corner at Club Six on Sixth Street.

SOUTHERN PACIFIC TRAIN STATION

Built to coincide with the Panama-Pacific
International Exposition of 1915

Original rail service down the peninsula had been initiated through a contract between railroad builders and taxpayers in San Francisco, San Mateo, and Santa Clara counties in 1863. The San Francisco and San Jose Railroad Company was consolidated into what would become the Southern Pacific Railroad in 1870. In 1912 the Southern Pacific Railroad broke ground on its new Mission Revival train station at Third and Townsend. *San Francisco Chronicle* reporters nervously interviewed railroad officials who assured the populace that the essential passenger depot serving the city would be ready in time for the Panama-Pacific International Exposition in 1915. Indeed, the depot was ready along with hundreds of streetcars, cable cars, automobiles, and horse-drawn jitneys to handle the crowd of about 8.6 million with ease. Passengers waited on five platforms serving eleven tracks, had access to telephones and telegraphs, and could use both pay and free restrooms. Along the way, they'd be enlightened by frescoes of mission scenes depicting the early settlement of California, in resonance with the building's architecture.

A statue of Willie Mays in front of AT&T Park now greets San Francisco Giants fans gathering before games in the vicinity of the old train station. In the 1970s, the old Southern Pacific station fell to the wrecking ball as former would-be passengers cruised by in their cars. A small shelter replaced it a block away. In almost a coup de grâce over the railroad, the empty space became a trailer park at first. Recently, the area has found new life in the redevelopment of the area around AT&T Park. Ridership had reached an all-time low on the Southern Pacific lines in the early 1970s, and the company petitioned the counties to abandon service altogether. The three counties that originally built the line all stepped up again and agreed to subsidize passenger fares to ensure that service continued. New ticket pricing stimulated ridership and set the stage for the state-run CalTrans to take over the line in 1980.

SOUTH PARK

George Gordon's oval park remains intact as a neighborhood meeting place

Left: San Francisco's elite called South Park home. The park in the center of the oval, shown here in 1865, was closed to all but the residents and their servants. Encroaching industrialization, which began at nearby Steamboat Point, drove the wealthy away. George Gordon conceived the idea of South Park in 1852. He planned to develop homes for fifty-eight families around a 550-foot oval park with a windmill at its center to provide water for the homes. He built the park in 1855 using parks in London, England, as inspiration. Seventeen mansions sprung up around the oval. The bottom fell out in 1869 when the "Second Street Cut" (see page 107) encouraged industrialization. Wealthier South Park denizens took to the hills, building homes on Nob Hill and Rincon Hill. The city took the park under its aegis in 1897. Nine years later, the earthquake and fire struck, destroying homes and driving residents away.

Above: George Gordon's oval park remains intact as a neighborhood meeting place. After the 1906 earthquake, the neighborhood was rebuilt as a light-industrial center. The park experienced a renaissance during the dot-com boom of the late 1990s, when low rents attracted entrepreneurs. So many start-up companies were set up here that some call South Park the dot-com revolution's ground zero. Around 500 people from surrounding businesses use the park as a lunch venue during the week, and families enjoy the park on weekends. The Friends of South Park received a $50,000 grant from the Park Renaissance Campaign. The money helped finance lighting fixtures and a water fountain, as well as picnic tables, benches, and trash receptacles. Volunteers from the Recreation and Parks Department's Youth Stewardship Program have installed two hummingbird gardens, created a new native plant garden, and refurbished the existing one.

FIRST STREET

The site of Thomas Selby's lead bullet
foundry with its 200-foot shot tower

Left: Thomas Selby constructed a lead-pipe and shot works at First
and Howard streets. The structure included a 200-foot-high shot
tower for the manufacture of lead bullets. Workers dropped molten
lead through a series of sieves into water below, creating the bullets.
This circa-1870 photograph looks down First Street to the shot
tower, which was one of the few tall structures to survive the 1906
earthquake. Selby was a forty-niner who came from New York and
began plying the merchant trade, specifically in importing metal and
hardware. In 1856 he founded the Selby Smelting and Lead Works, the
first attempt at large-scale metallurgy on the West Coast. His factory
employed fifty furnaces and soon became the largest consumer of
lead bullion in the United States. Travelers to San Francisco often
made a point of visiting the shot tower and metalworks strictly for
the entertainment value. Thomas Selby served as mayor from 1869
to 1871; he died of pneumonia in 1875.

Above: First and Howard streets now comprise part of the South of
Market, or SOMA, District. Much like Selby's shot tower, the area
south of Market Street had been given over to industrial uses up until
the last two decades. Factories, warehouses, and buildings that housed
dangerous or unpleasant materials were located along the coast and
south of the main shopping and residential neighborhoods. A form of
urban renewal took place in the late 1970s and continues to the present,
as formerly unproductive or undervalued properties were removed,
converted, or replaced. People primarily come here to work, with some
commuters spending hours in cars or trains to reach the city and its
high-paying, stable jobs. Rather than bullets, firms in the area are now
more likely to construct highly technical designs or media. Pacific Gas
and Electric's forerunner had its 160,000-cubic-foot gas tanks at this
corner in 1854, apparently across the street from Selby's furnaces, which
raged twenty-four hours a day. The gas plant was moved away in 1891.
In the distance of this view is the 345 California Center, or the "Tweezer
Towers" as it is locally known. This forty-eight-story skyscraper was
designed by Skidmore, Owings, and Merrill and completed in 1986.
At 695 feet, it is the third-tallest building in San Francisco after the
Transamerica Pyramid (853 feet) and 555 California Street (779 feet).

SECOND STREET

Rincon Hill was cut through to speed up deliveries to and from Steamboat Point

Left: China clippers of the Pacific Mail Steamship Line once docked at Steamboat Point at the intersection of today's Third and Berry streets. To reach the point from Mission and Market streets, horses had to pull cargo-laden wagons up Rincon Hill on Second Street. The steep hill became too much; in 1869 it was decided to cut through the hill to make the trip easier on both horses and teamsters. Photographers from Houseworth and Lawrence were on hand to record the progress. The area along the shore in the 1870s was a different place than it is today. At an ordinary high tide, water lapped the shore near today's Townsend, Eighth, and Sixteenth streets. Tidal creeks, called sloughs, meandered through nearby marshland that penetrated the coast to Mission Street between Seventh and Eighth streets, and Folsom Street between Fourth and Eighth streets.

Above: AT&T Park, home to the San Francisco Giants, dominates the landscape along San Francisco Bay at the foot of Second Street—it can be seen in the far distance of this view. The Giants play ball on a thirteen-acre site bounded by King, Second, and Third streets and China Basin. The first pitch was thrown against the Milwaukee Brewers in an exhibition game on March 31, 2000. The park is the heart of San Francisco's South Beach neighborhood—once home to the city's boatbuilding and ship repair industry—with its medium-density mixed-use blocks along the Embarcadero and King Street down to Third Street. Today's Steamboat Point, a development built in 1992 along the Embarcadero between King and Townsend streets, recalls the area's historic name. The clock tower at the center of the photo was built in 1907 for the Max Schmidt Lithograph Company. The building was renovated and transformed into 127 luxury apartments in the 1990s.

STEAMBOAT POINT

Kayakers gathered here in 2007 hoping to catch Barry Bonds's 756th home-run ball

Left: Steamboat Point, near the site of today's AT&T Park, stood along the shore at the foot of Rincon Hill. Much of the shoreline seen in this 1870 photograph has been filled in, creating the land southeast of King Street where the ballpark stands today. Steamboat Point formed the southern edge of Mission Bay and was an extremely popular place in San Francisco. Residents of the city received their mail from steamers tying up at this location beginning in the mid-1860s, near the intersection of today's Third and Berry streets. By that time, land speculators had already swallowed up most of the tideland lots under Mission Bay. In 1867 a causeway shut off most of the bay shipping interests. Industrial uses thrived in the vicinity, and efforts to fill the bay began with using it as a garbage dump.

Above: Near the place where men once abandoned boats in hopes of amassing a fortune by picking it off the ground, a century and a half later, men would amass boats there in an attempt to catch a fortune falling from the sky. AT&T Park, the city's grand urban stadium, adjoins McCovey Cove, where kayakers and ship captains just a few years ago gathered in hopes of catching one particular home-run ball before it fell in the drink. In 2007 San Francisco Giant Barry Bonds broke the all-time career home-run record in Major League Baseball. Speculation on when Bonds would hit the record-breaker quintupled ticket prices on the open market. On August 8, Bonds took number 756 to the bleachers in right-center field and boaters sighed in disappointment. The record-breaking ball garnered $750,000 at an auction.

CANDLESTICK POINT

The Beatles played their last commercial concert here on August 29, 1966

Above: When the City of San Francisco wanted to build a baseball stadium to host its new baseball team, the Giants, they went for the "cheap seats." City officials reportedly chose Candlestick Point because it was the least expensive land they could find. Construction is underway in this 1959 photograph. The stadium was ready for opening day on April 12, 1960; presidential candidate Richard Nixon tossed the ceremonial first pitch from the stands. The Oakland Raiders played their 1961 season here and the Beatles played their last live commercial concert at Candlestick Park on August 29, 1966. The Giants were set to meet the Oakland Athletics in the third game of the World Series on October 17, 1989, when the Loma Prieta earthquake struck. Candlestick Point derived its name from the nineteenth-century practice of burning abandoned ships in the nearby waters of the bay, which some said resembled lighted candlesticks.

Right: The park was renamed Monster Park in 2004 for its sponsor, Monster Cable, a maker of cables for electronic equipment. When the contract with Monster Cable expired in 2008, the stadium's name reverted to Candlestick Park. When the San Francisco 49ers began to play there in 1971, the stadium was enlarged and also enclosed in an effort to cut down the strong winds. Candlestick Park is the only National Football League stadium that began life as a baseball stadium. After the 1999 baseball season, the Giants moved to what is now AT&T Park. Since then, the 49ers have had the stadium to themselves. Plans to construct a new stadium at Candlestick Point have come to a standstill, and the 49ers are exploring the possibility of moving to Santa Clara, forty miles south of San Francisco.

CITY HALL

This San Francisco landmark underwent a $293 million earthquake retrofit in 1999

Left: This 1915 photograph of San Francisco's city hall reveals the shell of the building's dome, which is the fifth-largest in the world. The dome's niches contain favored nesting places for pigeons that apparently enjoy dropping in on the politicians. The city has gone so far as to recruit peregrine falcons to roust the rascals. The photograph was taken about two years after Mayor "Sunny Jim" Rolph broke ground for the new city hall, San Francisco's sixth. The three-year building project cost the city $3.5 million. The inset photo shows the previous city hall standing in utter ruin after the 1906 earthquake and fire. Shoddy workmanship, not repeated on the present city hall, was blamed for the building's demise. One wag said that, instead of mortar, a thin layer of corruption had held the building's bricks together.

Above: Like its predecessor, San Francisco's landmark city hall was unable to weather an earthquake, this one coming eighty-three years after the 1906 temblor. The body of President Warren Harding lay in state under the building's dome in 1923. (He died at the Palace Hotel on Market Street.) Joe DiMaggio married Marilyn Monroe here in 1954. In 1978 the building was the scene of a double murder when Dan White shot Mayor George Moscone and Supervisor Harvey Milk. The 1989 Loma Prieta earthquake left the building standing, but the structure was so badly damaged that it had to close. The building reopened almost ten years later on January 5, 1999, after undergoing a $293 million retrofit. As part of the retrofit, engineers installed shock absorbers in the form of 530 lead-rubber isolators.

ALAMO SQUARE

Alamo Square provides a front lawn for the Painted Ladies of Postcard Row

Left: At the time of their construction, these Alamo Square "Painted Ladies" houses were commonplace. The same designs, with decorative variations, can be found in any number of other neighborhoods and Bay Area cities. Machines invented during the industrial age, like the scroll saw, made mass production of decorative housing elements like brackets, spindles, patterned shingles, and other ornamentation easier. Victorian-era carpenters had access to new printed guidebooks to help them produce a house over and over again. During the decades between and during the World Wars, these Victorian creations were clad in war-surplus gray, brick, stucco, or, the ultimate embarrassment, aluminum siding. Nineteenth-century ostentation went against the new American disposition: that of a modern, streamlined, industrious, military giant. These homes were lucky to survive. An estimated 16,000 like them were demolished during the same period. Many others had decorative wooden elements removed and shipped off for the war effort.

Above: These six sisters on Steiner Street have been residing beside each other for almost 120 years now. Some credit San Francisco artist Butch Kardum with bringing color back to the Painted Ladies. He, along with several other artists in the mid-1960s, experimented with new, bright combinations of decoration on their Victorian homes, starting a trend locals call the colorist movement. The 1980s sitcom Full House featured the Painted Ladies from this memorable perspective during the opening credits. The show—and millions of other mass-media images—helped turn this particular view into a cultural icon for San Francisco. Local photographers complain about setting up their tripods in the grooves left behind in the grass by countless others taking the same shot. Some refer to the Painted Ladies as "Postcard Row." Alamo Square provides a front lawn for the ladies, and many in the neighborhood use the grassy spot with the perfect view for play, rest, or an afternoon stroll.

MISSION SAN FRANCISCO DE ASÍS / MISSION DOLORES

Built in 1776, Mission Dolores is the oldest surviving structure in San Francisco

Mission San Francisco de Asís (left) was founded June 29, 1776. The Spanish named their establishment for St. Francis of Assisi, the founder of the Franciscan order. Locals dubbed the place Mission Dolores for the nearby creek Arroyo de los Dolores, or "Creek of Sorrows"; the name stuck. The Mexicans ousted the Spanish from their country in 1821 and took possession of the missions in Alta California. Thirteen years later, in 1834, the Mexican government decided to close the missions and sell the land. Mission Dolores was the first on their list. In 1846 the Americans arrived and their priests settled in. By 1850 the area around the mission had become a popular place for horse racing, gambling, and drinking. The adjacent Mansion House in this photograph dates from that period—it served as a stagecoach stop for travelers to San Jose and beyond.

By the end of the nineteenth century, a growing population of Catholic immigrants were calling the mission their parish church. To make room, the Mansion House was torn down and replaced with a Gothic Revival brick church, which the 1906 earthquake destroyed. In 1913 construction began on the Mission Dolores Basilica. Four years later, architect Willis Polk supervised the restoration of the original adobe mission. The following year, in 1918, the first Mass was said in the new basilica. In 1926, on the heels of the Panama-California Exposition in San Diego's Balboa Park, the basilica's facade received a coat of Churrigueresque ornamentation in the Spanish Baroque style. In 1952 Pope Pius XII elevated Mission Dolores to the status of a minor basilica, making it the first basilica west of the Mississippi and only the fifth in the United States. The larger church is called Mission Dolores Basilica while the original adobe structure is still called by its historical name, Mission Dolores.

DOLORES PARK

In 1905 the city acquired the land that would become Dolores Park for $300,000

Above: Dolores Park, named for nearby Mission Dolores, was once the site of a Jewish cemetery. Congregation Sherith Israel used the property from 1861 to 1894. By 1900 the city's cemeteries were full and San Francisco passed a law stating that no further burials could be made in the city. Colma, about halfway down the peninsula, became the designated location. Thousands of bodies were moved to Colma, including those at soon-to-be Dolores Park. The city bought the property in 1905 at the whopping sum of $300,000 (about $4 million in today's currency). One of the city's warmest and sunniest microclimates, Mission Dolores turned out to be an ideal location for a park. But first, the former cemetery became a refuge for about 1,600 families displaced by the earthquake and fire. Temporary shacks erected in the park were occasionally saved and moved elsewhere in the city. A select few survive today. The far side of the park is dominated by Mission High School with its baroque tower.

Right: The park offers plenty of recreation to nearby residents in Noe Valley, the Mission, and the Castro. Facilities include a playground, two soccer fields, six tennis courts, and one basketball court. Members of the community have hosted some interesting events on its grasses over the years, including political rallies, festivals, Aztec ceremonial dances, and other performances. An interesting aspect of the park is that the J-Church light-rail line passes right through the park. Coming down Church Street and passing through the Market Street tunnel, the train cars, on reaching Eighteenth Street, had to enter the park where Church Street's grade became too steep. The train follows the former streetcar route laid out in the nineteenth century and returns to Church Street a few blocks farther south. The baroque dome in the center belongs to Mission High School; the distant spire is Mission Dolores.

CASTRO DISTRICT

The 1967 Summer of Love saw the Castro's birth as a gathering point for the gay community

Castro Street and its eponymous district remembers José Castro, who led the Mexican opposition to U.S. rule in California in the nineteenth century. He served as governor of Alta California from 1835 to 1836. The neighborhood now known as the Castro District was originally named Eureka Valley. In 1887 the Market Street Cable Railway brought the neighborhood to life when its streetcars began linking it to downtown. In the early part of the twentieth century, San Franciscans nicknamed Eureka Valley "Little Scandinavia" because so many people of Swedish, Norwegian, and Finnish descent lived there. Finilla's, a Finnish bathhouse dating from this period, stood behind the Café Flore on Market Street until 1986, and the Cove Diner on Castro Street was once called the Norse Cove. The 1967 "Summer of Love" saw the birth of the district as a gathering point for the gay community. The neighborhood gradually took on the name of the Castro District for the landmark theater on Market Street, seen here on the left.

The Castro District gained new attention with 2008's Oscar-winning movie *Milk*, about "the Mayor of Castro Street," gay activist Harvey Milk, who owned Castro Camera and was the first openly gay man to sit in city hall as a supervisor. Milk fell victim to Dan White's bullet at San Francisco's city hall in 1978. The heart of the district remains its immediately recognizable icon, the Castro Theatre with its Spanish Colonial Baroque facade. Its designer, Timothy L. Pflueger, also designed Oakland's Paramount Theater. While remembered for his theater designs, Pflueger accomplished much more. Other buildings by this prolific architect include the Transbay Terminal on Mission Street, the Top of the Mark on Nob Hill, and the San Francisco Stock Exchange Building on Sansome Street.

FILLMORE STREET

Fillmore's beloved arches were donated to the war effort in 1943

Left: To celebrate renewal after the 1906 earthquake and fire, denizens of Fillmore Street built fanciful arches on several of the street's downtown intersections. The city's Jewish families mostly relocated to Fillmore Street after the earthquake. They rebuilt Fillmore into a thriving commercial district and, until 1909, it served as the main street in the wasted metropolis. Fillmore merchants formed a neighborhood improvement association, and as one of their earliest acts in 1907 they erected the first arch. Festooned with a series of bulbs, the arch lit up the street like daytime whenever the merchants desired. As the commercial district expanded, fourteen arches in all were constructed from Fulton to Sacramento streets. The Fillmore District then earned a reputation as the most illuminated street in the country when the Panama-Pacific Exposition of 1915 brought pretty much everyone down the street and into the fair. As a part of the World War II effort, Fillmore residents pitched in and donated the beloved arches, removing them in 1943 (see inset).

Above: The culture of Fillmore slowly changed. Prior to the World Wars, Japanese American residents joined the neighborhood. When Japanese Americans were incarcerated during World War II, the Fillmore District became a vital African American community. During the war, available jobs drew many African Americans from the depressed South and across the nation. The Kaiser Shipyards was a large employer and paid well. A group of smart minority entrepreneurs soon opened round-the-clock entertainments for the workers who lived in the neighborhood. The sounds of bop, jazz, and the blues came from any number of restaurants, theaters, or nightclubs at any time of day or night. Since then the Fillmore District has bred generations of jazzmen and other musicians, earning the district a new moniker, "the Harlem of the West." During the 1960s, redevelopment of the district effectively muted the music for a few decades. But in recent years, the area has reclaimed its reputation as the place to hear great music and have a fun time.

TWIN PEAKS

Providing a 360-degree view of San Francisco and beyond

Left: Twin Peaks, a nearly identical pair of hills, rise 922 feet above sea level and provide a 360-degree view of San Francisco and beyond. The Spanish had a more colorful name for what they saw, naming the peaks Los Pechos de la Choca ("the Breasts of the Indian Maiden"). In 1901 a photographer from the San Francisco firm of Turrill and Miller set up a camera at the intersection of Twentieth and Noe streets to shoot this picture, which features a "Cook's Water" advertisement etched in white stone on the northern peak. The cross street just below where the photographer stood is Castro Street. Charles Beebe Turrill began working as an amateur photographer in 1886 and established a business around 1900 in San Francisco. "I am fighting to preserve the history of California—for the accuracy of historic records," he told the *San Francisco Call* in 1921.

Above: Homes and trees in the same view today show how the population has increased since 1901. Today, the name Twin Peaks applies not just to the look-alike hills but to the surrounding neighborhood as well. The Cook's Water advertisement is gone and the peaks now house the Summit Reservoir. Built in 1954 for the San Francisco Fire Department, the reservoir holds 14 million gallons of water. The department does not hold its liquid reserves back for fighting fires, however. Local residents tap into the resource to quench their thirst. The peaks remain largely undeveloped. The San Francisco Recreation and Parks Department manages the Twin Peaks Natural Area, which includes Eureka Peak (the south peak), Noe Peak (the north peak), and Christmas Tree Point, once the site of San Francisco's official Christmas tree. Twin Peaks is one of the few remaining habitats for the mission blue butterfly, an endangered species.

TWIN PEAKS BOULEVARD

Offering "a varied and pleasing panorama of ocean, bay, mountain, and metropolis"

Left: A photographer standing at Christmas Tree Point snapped a pair of vintage automobiles negotiating one of the hairpin turns on Twin Peaks Boulevard. The boulevard divides the two peaks and is the only road leading up to the summits. The street running in a straight line below is Market Street. That straight line is no accident; when Jasper O'Farrell laid out the city in 1847, he defined Market Street as a line aimed directly at the center of the peaks. The City of San Francisco built Twin Peaks Boulevard at a cost of $55,154. Construction on the boulevard began in 1915; automobiles began negotiating the hairpin turns one year later. City engineer M. M. O'Shaughnessy, who also designed the Twin Peaks Tunnel, laid out the boulevard. "From no other eminence in San Francisco can such a varied and pleasing panorama of ocean, bay, mountain, and metropolis be obtained," the *San Francisco Municipal Report* bragged in 1918.

Above: Twin Peaks Boulevard, which encircles its eponymous peaks in a broad figure eight, is little changed and today's adventurers can enjoy a ride on the very same road as the drivers of the vintage automobiles in the 1930s photograph. Tour buses chug up the boulevard, which is part of San Francisco's forty-nine-mile scenic drive, carrying tourists from all over the world. The buses compete for space with automobiles driven by visitors who also come to enjoy the view of the city below. Others come to hike the trails and watch the birds and other wildlife in the nature preserve that surrounds Noe and Eureka peaks. Here they can find the brush rabbit, the garter snake, and the California quail. Homes along the boulevard are highly prized commodities.

TWIN PEAKS TUNNEL

The convenience of the Muni Metro ushered in a new era of growth for the city

Above: Less cover and fewer houses better reveal the landscape around the west portal of the Muni Metro Twin Peaks Tunnel in this photograph from the early twentieth century. When it opened on February 3, 1918, it was one of the longest railway tunnels in the world. Land speculation gobbled up almost all of the 7,000 acres west of Twin Peaks while the tunnel was still under construction. The 2.27-mile tunnel cut twenty minutes off Sunset residents' commute times between Sloat Boulevard and Kearney Street downtown. The convenience ushered in a new era of growth for the city, as developers rapidly subdivided and set up housing tracts in advance, which became the neighborhoods of Forest Hill, West Portal, Balboa Terrace, St. Francis Wood, and Westwood Park. By the time the tunnel opened, $3 million worth of roads and an additional $3 million in new homes were built, waiting for that next generation of commuters. On the first trolleys rolling west rode the first tenants, ready to take possession. Merchants came soon after.

Right: The former sand dunes west of Twin Peaks became bedroom retreats for Financial District professionals and by 1924 the assessed value of these lands grew astronomically. These neighborhoods became the city's first gated communities, exclusive retreats with homeowner associations that practiced racist restrictions and strict maintenance schedules. Somehow, early on, a certain number of pedestrians and automobile drivers missed the message that the tunnel was intended for trolleys only, and a few accidents occurred. Six years following the tunnel's opening, local economists declared the project a success. The value of the 7,000 acres west of Twin Peaks had increased by about $4 million. Taxes collected from the region over the six years totaled $92,000. Since the 1910 census of 416,912 people, the city's population has roughly doubled, with the largest increases coming from the neighborhoods between the ocean and Twin Peaks. Now, of course, the neighborhoods welcome all who can afford them and recently have enjoyed a sort of revitalization as a new generation of professionals has moved in.

GOLDEN GATE PARK'S
CONSERVATORY OF FLOWERS

North America's oldest existing public conservatory

Left: When the city acquired this grand conservatory, it was still in boxes from the estate of businessman James Lick. Lick had a certain genius. He arrived in San Francisco in 1848 and brought $30,000 in gold. He invested in land in sleepy Yerba Buena, a town of a few hundred. About a month later, gold was discovered and his investment multiplied overnight. Lick liked grand ostentation. He built an observatory on the peak of nearby Mount Hamilton. He desired an impressive conservatory of the world's plants on his estate. He'd ordered the parts to build it, but they were still in storage when he died. Wealthy city residents bought the pieces and donated them to the city. Once assembled, the building opened in 1879. Four years later, in 1883, a boiler explosion and fire completely destroyed the main dome. Railroad magnate Charles Crocker donated the money to restore it. This photograph shows visitors enjoying the restored Conservatory of Flowers in 1897.

Above: The Conservatory of Flowers survived the 1906 earthquake intact, but the Crocker restoration was just one of a series of repairs and reconstructions performed on the building over the years. The most recent, a $25 million restoration, took place in 1999 after a severe windstorm damaged the building. Four years later, the building reopened with a grand celebration. The mission of the conservatory carries on to this day and has earned it the position as North America's oldest existing public conservatory. The building contains about 1,700 species of plants from more than fifty countries. Among the ongoing exhibits are collections of aquatic plants, lowland and highland tropical plants, and potted plants. The conservatory also features seasonal or special exhibits, guided tours for adults, an educational program for schoolchildren, and reception halls for weddings.

HAIGHT STREET LOOKING WEST FROM ASHBURY

Named for exchange banker Henry Haight and politician Munroe Ashbury

Above: This photograph of Haight Street looking west from Ashbury was taken in the 1930s, some thirty years before the 1967 Summer of Love made the street and the district famous. These two streets bear the names of early San Francisco leaders: exchange banker Henry Haight and politician Munroe Ashbury, who sat on the Board of Supervisors from 1864 to 1870. Some argue that Haight Street was named for Henry's nephew and namesake, California governor Henry Haight. When he served as governor, the younger Haight appointed Ashbury to the first San Francisco Park Commission. Before the Haight Street Cable Railroad arrived in 1883, scattered farms dotted the sand dunes. The cable-car turnaround at Haight and Stanyan streets dropped passengers at the end of the line. Some came to watch baseball at the Haight Street Grounds, others to have fun at the Paul Boynton Chute Company's amusement park. Some liked what they saw, bought property, and put down roots. By 1910 developers had stepped in and houses covered the landscape.

Right: Haight Street at Ashbury still serves as the center point of the district. Tourists continue to visit the Haight-Ashbury District to see where the Summer of Love began at the summer solstice in 1967. When the hippies arrived in droves in the mid-1960s, stores opened to accommodate their eccentric needs. The first was the Psychedelic Shop at 1535 Haight Street, just down from Ashbury. Psychedelia can still be found if one looks close enough. The Queen Anne–style home at 710 Ashbury Street still stands with its bay windows and Victorian-era decoration hiding its role as the place where the Grateful Dead once lived. The house continues to draw flocks of pilgrims, most of them "Deadheads," die-hard Grateful Dead fans. Eclectic boutiques and ethnic restaurants have replaced most other signs of that unique summer, however.

CORNER OF HAIGHT AND ASHBURY STREETS

Center of the 1967 Summer of Love

Jerry Garcia, lead guitarist and San Francisco native, and Phil Lesh, bassist of the would-be Grateful Dead, stand at the corner of Haight and Ashbury streets during the 1960s, perhaps about the time they changed their name from the Warlocks. "The Dead," as they're affectionately known, led almost a religious crusade of music across the world, bringing the sounds of 1967's Summer of Love and the spirit of peace, love, and harmony to millions. A crowd of Deadheads, perpetually nomadic concertgoers, followed the band in a caravan everywhere they could, trusting in the communal spirit of the era to care for their human needs. For three decades the Grateful Dead represented the San Francisco hippie counterculture to the rest of America, helping to define an era. In their many years onstage, the group explored all of their influences blues, improvisational jazz, country and western, bluegrass blending them into a sound called psychedelic rock.

This famous intersection became known as the place where young people from around the world came in search of love and peace. Visitors are still drawn to this bohemian corner of San Francisco, but today they are more likely to be sightseeing, searching out the impressive Victorian houses that still surround the area, and buying ice cream from the nearby Ben and Jerry's store. Although the area is more gentrified these days, it still retains many independently run bars, restaurants, clothing boutiques, and music stores. Jerry Garcia died in 1995; the surviving members of the band—Phil Lesh, Bob Weir, and Mickey Hart—continued the Grateful Dead tradition under their former name, the Other Ones. In 2003 the group changed its name to the Dead.

TWELFTH AVENUE AND QUINTARA STREET

Giant sand dunes have become a neighborhood

A steam shovel and dump trucks were busy transforming sand dunes into what would become a neighborhood at Twelfth Avenue and Quintara Street in this March 2, 1927, photo. The Parkside Realty Company had begun developing this part of town in 1909. Around the same time, a city street renaming commission was appointed. The commission planned an alphabetical list of names for east–west streets parallel to Golden Gate Park taken from some of the city's Spanish founding families. The avenues ran north–south and were numbered. Once the names went public, the commission met with a litany of opposition for the names they chose, especially here in the Sunset District, where the first residents had just settled into their new homes. While everyone liked the alphabetical pattern, a certain sense of nationalism and "Lincoln-fever" struck the area. These residents wanted some American-sounding names on the list, so the main road passing by the park became Lincoln Way, the fourth street in town named for Abraham Lincoln.

The alphabetical pattern of names starts north of Golden Gate Park with Anza, Balboa, and Cabrillo. The park and the streets bordering it interrupt the pattern, but south of the park, Irving, Judah, Kirkham, and Lawton represent the American names local residents insisted on in 1909. The list then continues with the commission's Spanish names: Moraga, Noriega, Ortega, Pacheco, Quintara, Rivera, Santiago, Taraval, Ulloa, Vicente, and Wawona. The list of Spanish names featured many of the same from the roll call of the Anza expedition, which founded the first European settlements on the San Francisco peninsula in 1776. The western neighborhoods today are studded with enclaves of young urban professionals. The architecture of Sunset Heights retains some turn-of-the-century charm distinctive from blocks farther west. Quintara and Twelfth Avenue is near Sunset Heights Park, which was created in 1910.

ADOLPH SUTRO'S PUBLIC BATHS

In 1980 the site became part of the Golden Gate National Recreation Area

Adolph Sutro opened his eponymous baths in 1896, the same year he christened the second Cliff House. The baths were so famous that Thomas Edison visited the following year and filmed San Franciscans "taking the waters." The baths had seven swimming pools to accommodate up to 10,000 people at a time. Altogether, the pools held 1.7 million gallons of water and could be filled in one hour by high tides. The pools' waters were set at different temperatures, ranging from ice-cold to steaming hot. Visitors could swing on trapezes, skim down slides, leap from springboards, and soar through the air from a high dive. For a nominal rental fee, a swimmer could take the waters wearing one of the bath's 20,000 bathing suits and dry off with one of the 40,000 available towels. The Sutro Baths fell victim to the 1906 earthquake, as the glass walls proved too fragile for the temblor. Various twentieth-century attempts to revive the baths failed.

The Sutro Baths are gone, apparently never to be replaced. They burned in 1966, leaving the empty shell we still see today. Stagnant pools of water stand where San Franciscans once bathed. In 1952 Sutro's grandson grew tired of losing money every year, so he sold the baths to George Whitney, owner of Playland at the Beach, for $250,000. Whitney was not able to properly maintain the baths' intricate pumping system; he closed the baths in 1966. Soon after, the revered structure burned in what many called a suspicious fire. A developer stepped in with plans for homes and a shopping center on the site. In 1980 the National Park Service put an end to all that, purchasing the property for $5 million and adding the site of the famous baths to the Golden Gate National Recreation Area.

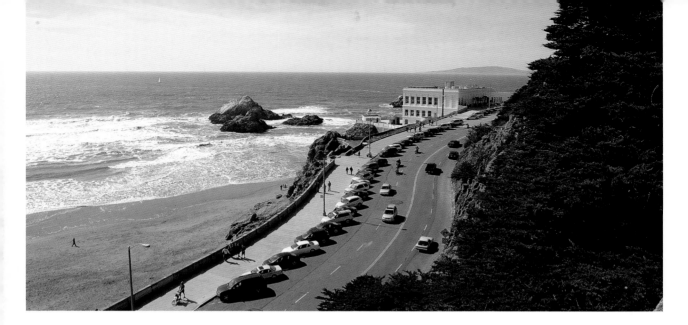

CLIFF HOUSE

Only the highest class of visitor could afford to dine at the Cliff House

Left: Most photographs of the Cliff House show Adolph Sutro's 1896 version in all its Victorian splendor. This one shows the first Cliff House that Senator John Buckley and C. C. Butler built in 1863. Only the highest class of visitor could afford to dine at the Cliff House in those days—not due to the price of meals, but because of transportation. Toll fees on Point Lobos Road or a strong enough team of horses to take a rider over the rolling dunes west of town cost fifty cents—half a week's pay for most. Ulysses S. Grant visited in 1879, and Rutherford B. Hayes ate there in 1890. By then, public transportation had improved for the workingman and wealthier clientele moved to other, more exclusive resorts. Some reported that the Cliff House had become "a den of gamblers and prostitutes." In 1881 Sutro tried to fix that reputation. His new Cliff House offered educational exhibits of natural artifacts for families. The photographer timed this shot perfectly, capturing a tall ship just entering the Golden Gate.

Above: Today the Cliff House serves much the same purpose it did in the 1890s. It remains a picturesque place to have a meal or host a celebration. In 1887 a ship crashed into the rocks and exploded off the shore, damaging the building. In 1894 a more mundane kitchen fire leveled the place. Sutro's palatial new Cliff House, a five-story Victorian masterpiece, lasted just eleven years before it too burned. By 1909 a much less ostentatious building went up on the site. It was a place people visited on their way to fairs in the 1920s and 1930s, where men had their final drink before shipping off to war in the 1940s, and served as a way station along the highway in the 1950s. In 1969, for the first time in almost a century, the Cliff House closed up. Jointly operated by private restaurant owners and the National Park Service since 1977, the Cliff House is now back to its old grandeur, hosting gala affairs, offering gourmet meals, and, as always, providing an impressive place to view the Pacific Ocean.

OCEAN BOULEVARD AND THE SURF
FROM SUTRO HEIGHTS.

OCEAN BEACH

Ocean Beach's sandy terrain stretches for more than three miles south to Fort Funston

Left: Horsecars first carried visitors to the shore of the Pacific Ocean just below the Cliff House and Sutro Baths. The area became such an attraction that a park with amusements and concessions sprang up along the beach. George Whitney and his brother Leo stepped in, and by the time the 1920s were roaring, Playland at the Beach appeared. The amusement park thrived during the 1930s and 1940s. Visitors could forget the Great Depression and World War II for just a little while. Arthur Looff set up the Bob Sled Dipper roller coaster, which everyone affectionately called "the Bobs," in 1921. The next year, he added the Big Dipper. Other rides included Shoot-the-Chutes, a carousel, a Ferris wheel, the Aeroplane Swing, the Dodge-Em, the Ship of Joy, Noah's Ark, and the Whip. The pair of Dutch-style windmills in the photograph was built at the edge of Golden Gate Park in 1903 to help provide water to the park.

Above: Today's Ocean Beach begins at the Cliff House, where some people enjoy lunch or dinner in the restaurant above the rocks while others are on the beach hoping to hook a fish. Ocean Beach's sandy terrain stretches about three and a half miles south to Fort Funston, once home to Battery Richmond P. Davis, which had guns with a maximum range of more than twenty-six miles. Between the Cliff House and the fort, people enjoy themselves by playing volleyball, walking along the esplanade, and flying kites. Some folks will brave the waters to bodyboard or surf. Swimming is discouraged, however. Signs warn of rip currents—swift-moving channels of water that rush from the shore out to sea and carry anything (and anybody) along with them.